MORRISSEY
ALONE
AND
PALELY
LOITERING

PHOTOGRAPHY BY
KEVIN CUMMINS

 CASSELL
ILLUSTRATED

CONTENTS

INTRODUCTION

This book is a celebration of photography and Morrissey.

I first photographed Morrissey in 1983, and the majority of the pictures included in this book cover the timespan from that year through to 1994. Included here also is a series of contemporary portraits exploring the ongoing devotion that Morrissey inspires in his fans, which I have taken as I have travelled around the world meeting people with themed tattoos of their hero. These two things are inextricably linked. Morrissey would not be the cultural figure he is today without his fans. As I state in this book, I have photographed many different musicians but the relationship between Morrissey and his fans appears to me to be a truly unique one.

It doesn't surprise me that Morrissey has become such a prominent cultural figure. I was always a fan and knew immediately that The Smiths had something different to say and something special to offer. Visually, Morrissey was also different from other musicians. He always collaborated with me fully and would come to photo shoots full of ideas. Morrissey has had an astonishing career as a solo musician and I am pleased that I was at Wolverhampton to capture his first concert after the demise of The Smiths. The series of photographs taken there shows the excitement and chaos that reigned at his first live performance in over two years.

There are four main themes in this book that emerge both visually and textually. For the first time, I have written extensively about the art of photography: my influences, how a photograph works, how images can be read, and the absolute importance of visual culture. I have also written about portraiture alongside the studio shots of Morrissey, explaining what makes an articulate portrait and sharing some stories of working directly with Morrissey on some of my better-known images. Additionally, I have also discussed live photography: how it has changed in recent years and the challenges that face a professional photographer working in the unpredictable, if somewhat exciting, environment of the live concert. The book includes photographs from various Morrissey tours – at venues in Dublin and Cologne, Japan and the United States, as well as places in the UK. Finally, in an essay by Gail Crowther, the significance of fans using their bodies as sites of devotion is explored to accompany the photographs of Morrissey-inspired tattoos that I have taken over the last five years. Why do fans have this deep level of devotion to him, and why might they use their skin as a permanent expression of this love?

The process of revisiting my archive and looking through old frames for this book has been deeply rewarding. Not only can I see how the significance of portraits as historical documents has changed over time, but I was also able to appreciate fully the scope of my work with Morrissey. When I photographed The Smiths for the first time at Dunham Massey, Greater Manchester, for the *NME*, it was commissioned as a cover feature. Unfortunately, the features editor changed his mind at the last minute and put Big Country on the cover, telling me that he felt The Smiths would never be big enough to be on the cover of the *NME*. Since that ill-judged pronouncement I have shot more than half a dozen Morrissey covers for the *NME*, as well as countless book jackets. One of the photographs from that first Smiths session is now in the permanent collection of London's National Portrait Gallery and the shot of Morrissey that I envisaged for the cover has since been used in numerous magazines, on book covers and on a variety of merchandise worldwide. In fact, visually Morrissey has such a strong iconography today that often you do not need to see his face in a photograph to know that it is him – just a quiff in silhouette or flowers hanging out of the back pocket of his jeans. Even just the backdrop of an empty stage, such as a large portrait of Edith Sitwell or Harvey Keitel, means that the venue is unmistakably Morrissey's. Building this visual mythology was one of my main aims when photographing Morrissey, and he was one of the few musicians I have worked with who fully understood how and why this was important.

Ultimately, though, this is a book about time, permanence and devotion. Photography, really, in all of its forms is about permanence in one way or another. Things and people come and go. Morrissey and his fans are captured here and preserved in a time that is gone forever. But their connection, those rare, brief moments of meeting, can be revisited, visually at least.

So, paradoxically, this book is about loss and reanimation. And love, too.

THE SMITHS
1983–1986

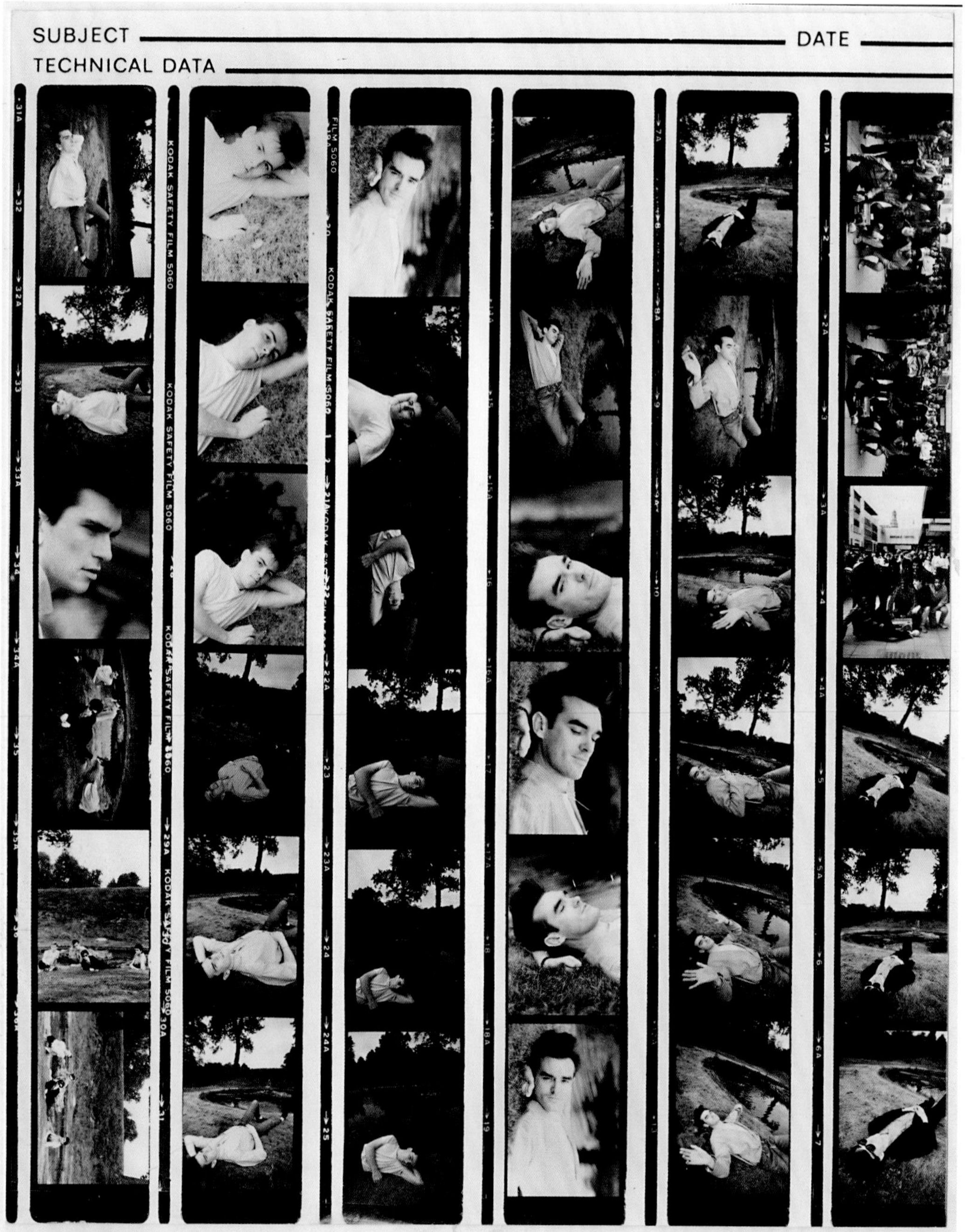
SUBJECT
DATE
TECHNICAL DATA
KODAK SAFETY FILM 5060

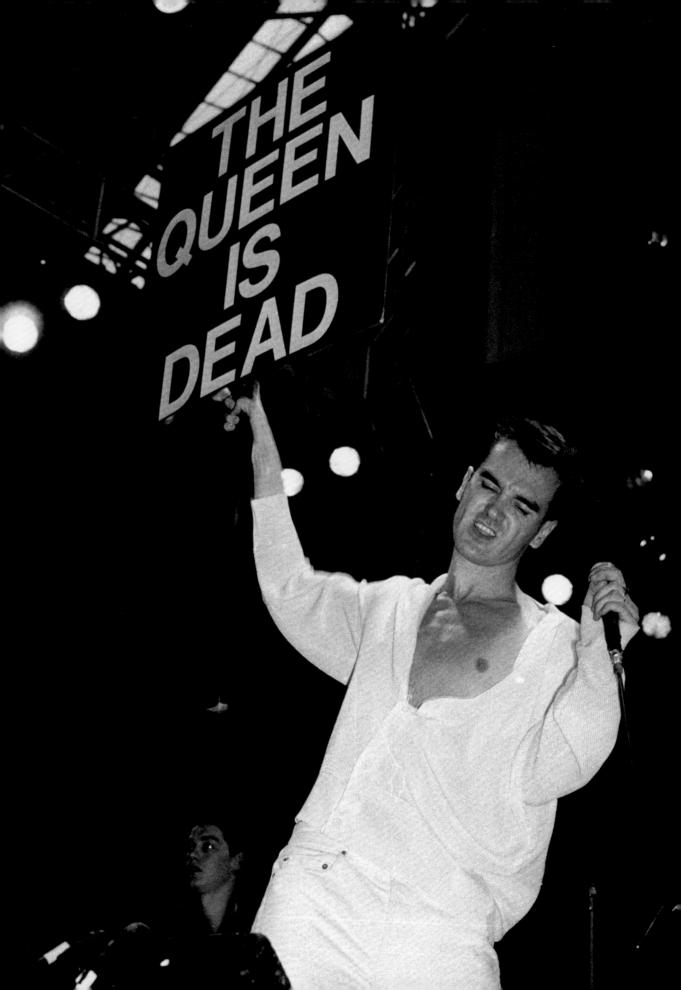

THE SMITHS CONVENTION

MUSING ON PHOTOGRAPHY

"The only way to kill death is through photography"

—JEAN COCTEAU

Photography is a melancholy art. The process of seeing, framing and capturing an image does not happen just by chance. It requires skill, training and a certain amount of intuition. The melancholy, I suppose, comes in freezing a moment that is then forever gone. As Roland Barthes said, "Every photograph is a certificate of presence." But what once *is* will one day be undone. That said, I do not really agree with Barthes that photography is all about death. For me, my photographs are about celebrating life; preserving a fraction of time, and from that creating iconography.

I am mostly known for photographing musicians, but, oddly, when I started my studies at Salford in 1971 I was fairly indifferent to music photography. I wanted to be a portrait photographer. Although perhaps I didn't see it at the time, there was a theme to my interests and inspirations: the lonely and dispossessed captured by the lens of Diane Arbus were elevated from the marginalized to the powerful; August Sander's portraits, stark and Germanic, focused on the abject in society, circus performers in caravans occupying urban wastelands; Bill Brandt and his social commentary on all aspects of British society, the wet, cobbled backstreets of Halifax and the abstract uses of shadow and light. Later, photojournalists such as Denis Thorpe at the *Guardian* captured my imagination, too, documenting the miners' strike and the riots at Strangeways; and Jane Bown at the *Observer*,

who worked almost exclusively in black and white, using the natural light that was available. It was a potent mix of visual influences that established a particular way of looking at the world, along with specific techniques of capturing it. The poetics of photography were beginning to be established for me, and Susan Sontag's words resonated:

Photography is about seeing your subject as they never see themselves, having knowledge of them that they can never have. But it is also about playing a part in someone's mortality and vulnerability. Portrait photography is about looking and being looked at.

My interest in photography was established at a fairly young age. My father and my maternal grandfather were both keen amateurs. We had a darkroom in our house (essentially a cupboard), and my grandfather had a darkroom in his cellar. On my fifth birthday I was given a box camera and my father showed me how to process and print my own pictures. Even then I was captured by the magic of the darkroom, by the smell of the chemistry and by the fascination of visual creation. Sometimes with my dad, sometimes alone, I would play around with techniques such as overlaying film, solarization, photograms – the techniques of Man Ray and the Surrealists. I became keen on the whole process of photography. This interest began to wane a little in my early to mid-teenage years, though in part because we were not taught photography at school. Instead,

I became interested in architecture and urban drawing. Although this seemed a move away from my first love, in fact I believe our early influences can sit and bubble away in our imaginations. It is probably no coincidence that much of my photography tends to have an urban setting.

I was drawn back to taking photographs in my late teens for a number of reasons. First, all around me Salford was being demolished. This was documented eloquently by Shirley Baker, who over a number of years produced a series of images depicting the forgotten piles of bricks, the rubble and dirt, children playing on building sites, and the diverse communities. I felt an important part of my own history was being wiped away and would soon vanish, so I started to photograph it before it disappeared for good. Second, as I started Sixth Form it also felt as if the end of my secondary education was looming, and as we were then in our final schooldays together, I began to take photographs of my friends. I suppose both of these things are about loss and the desire to preserve or somehow reanimate.

Following this, I suddenly started to take photography seriously, and this coincided with a timely meeting that even now feels a little otherworldly. Aged 16, I worked at the Queen's Hotel, in Manchester, waiting on tables. One evening, the head waiter introduced me to an elderly man who ate his supper there once a month. It was L S Lowry. I was presented to him as a "young man who wanted to study photography". The problem I had was that I never felt "the arts" were for people like me, from a working-class background; it felt like the preserve of the middle classes. People like me got a degree and would then go back into education to teach. Lowry gave me some straightforward advice – always follow your dreams – and then I asked him to sign the menu for me. I wouldn't say it was *the* moment that changed me, but it was pretty important, as was Lowry's visual influence. For the first time I understood that it was possible to observe what was around you – ordinary scenes and places, streets, factories, bridges, people – and turn them into something else. For want of a better word, "art".

For many of us our teenage years are a formative time when we are exposed to a whole range of influences and ideas. I was no exception. It can be hard to unravel your own unconscious influences, or even understand the ways in which ideas can bubble away for a time, only to erupt later. For the next few years I would be surrounded by things that I now see played a part in my development as a photographer. The strongest early influence would certainly have been religion. I went to Catholic church until I was 12, stopped for a while, and then returned again during Sixth Form. At the same time, in literature classes (in a Catholic grammar school) we were reading mostly white, male, Catholic writers such as Graham Greene.

The iconography of Catholicism is something that I still love to this day, and I visit churches and cathedrals wherever I travel. The lighting, the candles, the tortuous poses, the plush decadence of Catholic imagery. I see now that my photograph of Richey Edwards, his upper body stamped with images of Marilyn Monroe, could not have happened without my Catholic sensibility. And there was a kind of meta narrative going on, a send-up of the very iconography that I was using.

At this time I was also immersed in the kitchen-sink dramas and soap operas of the 1950s and 1960s – *Billy Liar, Coronation Street, Room at the Top, A Taste of Honey* – many of the same influences cited by Morrissey. They said something to me about my life and I think their impact shows in my pictures, too – the way I prefer to use natural light, and my preference for locating people in a setting that suits them. By the time I reached college age, I had become interested in strong female figures. Based on my love of Diane Arbus, a friend suggested that I read *The Bell Jar* by Sylvia Plath, which took me out of the streets of Manchester to the impossible glamour of New York. With the main character, Esther Greenwood, there was the continuing theme of loneliness and isolation; the person who never quite fits in. This connected back to Arbus, who was a strong visual presence during my college years. Above my desk I had a reproduction of her photograph depicting two seven-year-old twin sisters, Cathleen and Colleen Wade (*Identical Twins, Roselle, New Jersey, 1967*). I love the symmetry of the picture. The girls are wearing identical clothes and headbands, and I was impressed by the composition. Arbus shot this in a square aspect ratio, always a challenge but especially for portraiture. The image toys with identity issues of sameness and difference and leaves the viewer uneasy. Even today, I feel a sense of disquiet looking at the photograph.

Also at this time I began watching lots of films. At college, a group of us would go to the cinema each week. Two films that I believe had a direct impact on how I shoot my photographs were *A Clockwork Orange* and *Cabaret*. Stylistically and content-wise, I see traces of both of these films in my work – the glossy veneer hiding the tackiness lurking just beneath the surface, and the wide shots of urban alienation, of underpasses and backstreets.

Like the anarchic, chaotic style of *A Clockwork Orange*, people have said to me that my photographs break all the rules of composition. And often they do – but this, I believe, is one reason why they work. You can be technically brilliant but have no soul. The same thing happens in music, too, I think. If you take The Smiths, they may not have all been virtuosos but when they played together, the chemistry of it worked, and that is why you could not replicate it in any other way. Photographs are like that, too. You have to consider the emotion of a picture and then try to give something more to the viewer.

I often shoot in black and white, which makes the viewer work harder. People see the world in colour, so it requires less work to look at or interpret a colour image. Initially, I thought colour was amateur. I didn't really like it and I never studied it properly, so it took me a while to learn how to use it. The magazines that I read used black and white, and the television I watched was black and white, so as a consequence I thought in black and white. As a photographer it does make shooting more difficult because you have to understand how light works. I would see large patches of monochrome and then have to be aware of how the tonal range would work in this. On a more prosaic level, at the start of my career colour film was more expensive, and the magazines I was commissioned by published only in black and white. If I had shot Joy Division on that bridge in colour, nobody would have used it.

The decision to shoot in colour or black and white also plays a part in the story that my photographs tell. My aim is to create striking iconography. And if you work repeatedly with the same person this is easier to achieve; you not only build a rapport but you also understand how a visual identity will work for them and how they will be viewed. I'm not just recording what passes in front of my camera, I'm helping the viewer to understand the importance and stature of the musician they've emotionally invested in. You have to create this via composition. Yes, you might be fixing them within the boundaries of the image, but you create the frame for that to happen. In this sense, I think photography can play a part both in capturing and creating a cultural memory. A photograph is, after all, one way of catching a moment of truth – a fleeting moment, a fraction of a second. But, once it is fixed, it can then seep into the cultural consciousness. You can know how to "see" a band, and in some cases, if an image is powerful enough, it can even give you an idea of what a band will sound like.

The relationship between photography and truth, though, is quite a slippery one. It would be fair to say that there is no absolute truth within the frame of a photograph, and this is something Susan Sontag believed: photography is about lots of things, but least of all the truth. While I wouldn't go that far, I do think at best a photograph offers a version of the truth. You give parts of the story within the frame and the viewer doesn't need to know anything outside of that. When I photographed Morrissey alongside a handwritten sign saying "Penis mightier than the sword", you don't as a viewer need to know about all the other people present in the room when that shot was taken. When I photographed Ian Curtis leaning against the rehearsal-room wall in Manchester, the wall behind him looks black and he looks alone and rather serious. It doesn't matter that in fact the wall was brown and the rest of the band were around him telling jokes and trying to make him laugh. The reality of the photograph is that, in that second, this was the story the image was telling. Therefore, although it's a truth, it's also partly manipulative; you are guiding the viewer to see which part of the photo is important by the way you compose the image.

This in turn, I think, shows the ways in which photography is connected to fantasy. Although as a photographer I can manipulate an image, ultimately I have no control over how it is read. This doesn't bother me because I think often people can project what they want to see into an image. Morrissey becomes what people want him to be. If I take a picture of Morrissey with his shirt off, that, too, feeds into the way he is read. Photographs can be about yearning or desire or even longing. Sontag described this really well when she wrote in *On Photography*:

> *A photograph is both a pseudo-presence and a token of absence. Like a wood fire in a room, photographs – especially those of people, of distant landscapes and faraway cities, of the vanished past – are incitements to reverie. The sense of the unattainable that can be evoked by photographs feeds directly into the erotic feelings of those for whom desirability is enhanced by distance.*

But I do think they are incitements to reverie as well, and this is a good way to describe how images age over time. They may begin in a particular cultural or historical moment, but how they resonate and are read changes. An image may have a completely different meaning ten or fifteen years after it was taken. If a person dies, it may have more poignancy. As people age, an image capturing someone at the height of their physical beauty becomes a statement on ageing and mortality. The meaning behind them differs and can alter. An image may inspire nostalgia or a sense of loss, but equally it can reanimate and celebrate.

I think it can be hard to understand why some photographs inspire this reverie and others do not. Barthes talks about a *punctum* – the idea that every image has a particular feature that pierces us, but what this might be and how it works is pretty mysterious. I think context is probably quite important. If you look at an image of Ian Curtis knowing he is dead, you might read it differently. Equally, looking at a picture of someone you care about is likely to inspire stronger emotions. Or, on a more political level, an image of a child in Vietnam running toward the camera covered in napalm is going to inspire a powerful reaction. Maybe to understand how photography works, you have to think about its purpose as well, and like any medium you can use it for a number of purposes. It can document things; it can be used for newsgathering; you can capture friends, family, loved ones. In fact, you can create just about anything. Historically, it is a fairly new medium – and its digital incarnation even newer. I use photography to create iconography, and it seems to me that this creation is a combination of both skill and intuition. Because intuition is a bit intangible, perhaps this is where the mystery that Barthes writes about comes from. Composition isn't just happenstance, it's intuitive. I'm left-handed, so I probably balance a shot compositionally in a different way from a right-handed photographer. Vantage point, frame and focus are equally as important. This forms the visual *gestalt* of a photo. But intuition is difficult to explain, or even describe. And often things feel a bit beyond intuition anyway. I like to use my own camera because it becomes such a part of me that it feels as though it isn't there. I know how it balances, how to hold it. It's not even like an extension; it literally becomes unseen, unfelt, just somehow *there*. You can't teach this, and it's difficult to explain, but I do think it can highlight some of the mysteries about the art of photography. There's so much we can't know or predict.

When I took some of my best-known photographs, I could not have predicted that they would have the cultural life they have since taken on. Over the years I have become more confident as a photographer, less shy and more comfortable. In my early days I didn't direct people because it was easier just to let them do what they wanted. But now I'm happier to give instructions or collaborate on an image, as I did many times with Morrissey. On reflection, I can look at photographs that I took in my early years, such as of Joy Division on the bridge, and know everything that is "wrong" with it and how I would shoot it now. The danger there is that, if it was technically perfect, it might not be the picture that it is. Perhaps it is its naive charm that works. I guess we'll never know.

Barthes claimed that there are three aspects to photography: to do, to undergo and to look. Then there are the three roles of the people involved: the photographer, the referent and the spectator. It is all about the gaze, really. Yet Barthes says photography usually fails to capture that elusive "something" of a person; the self remains like a giggling imp that can't be pinned down. That is why I love portraiture. How does meaning get into the image? Why can some pictures be so melancholic, and why do certain photographs refuse to give up their secrets? For Sontag:

Photography is an elegiac art, a twilight art. Most subjects photographed are, just by virtue of being photographed, touched with pathos.

In this book, these portraits celebrating Morrissey achieve, I hope, this elegiac quality.

WOLVERHAMPTON
DECEMBER 1988

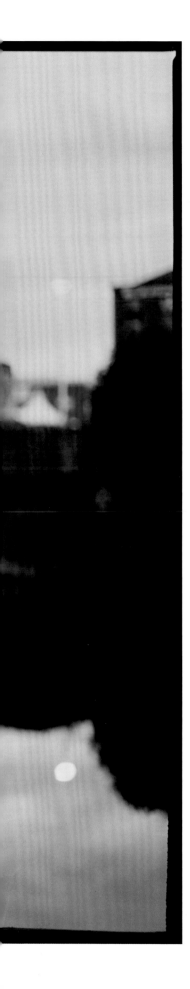

KODAK TMY 6053   KODAK TMY 6053   KODAK TMY 6053
TMY▷9
TMY▷8
TMY▷7
TMY▷6
KODAK TMY 6053   KODAK TMY 6053   KODAK TMY 6053
6053

KOD'AK TMX 6052
TMX ▷ 5
KOD'AK TMX 6052
TMX ▷ 4
KOD'AK TMX 6052
KOD'AK TMX 6052
TMX ▷ 3
KOD'AK TMX 6052
KOD'AK TMX 6052
TMX ▷ 2
KOD'AK TMX 6052
KOD'AK TMX 6052
TMX ▷ 1

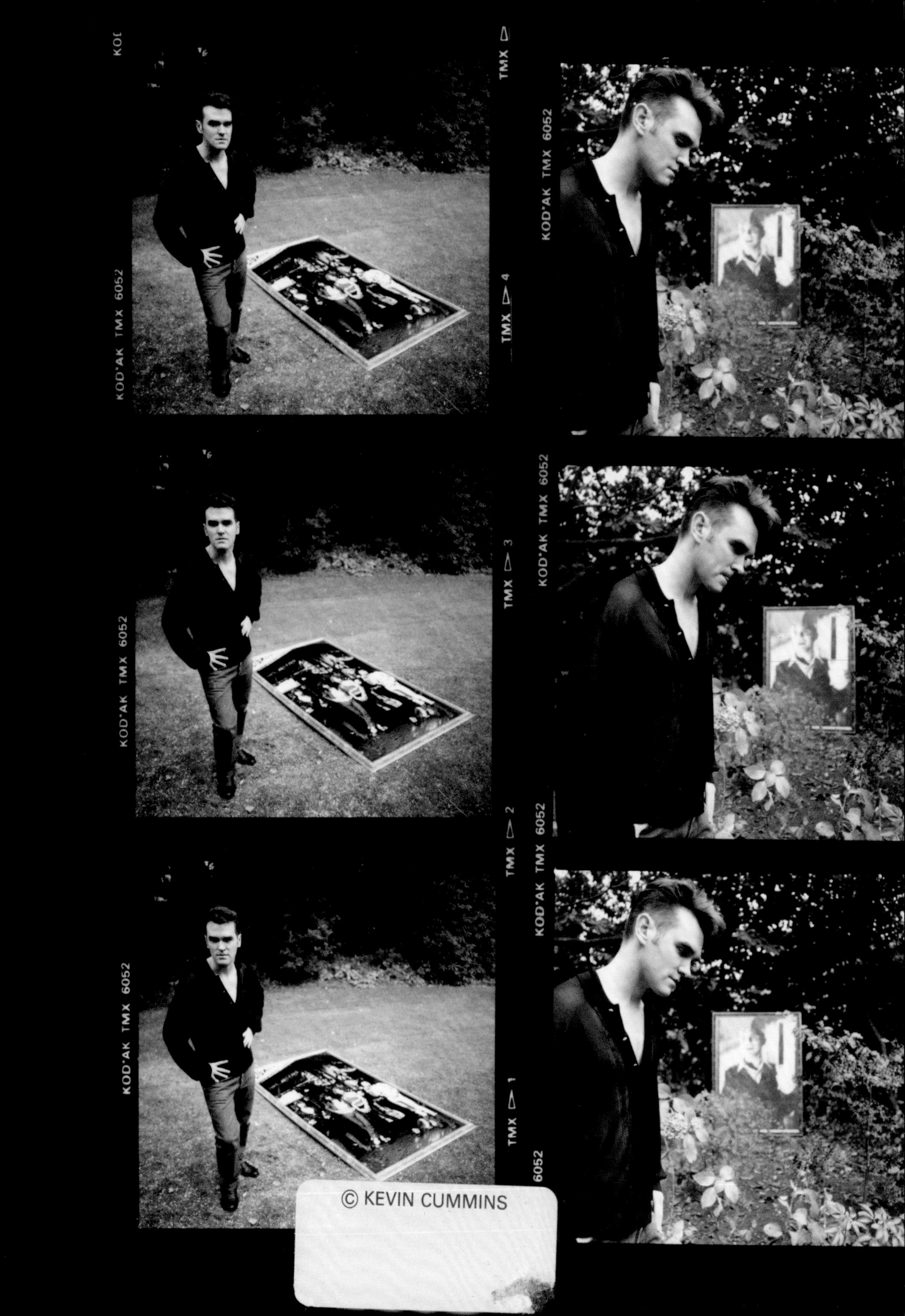
© KEVIN CUMMINS

ON PORTRAITS

*"We've all got an identity. You can't avoid it.
It's what you've got when you take everything else away."*
—DIANE ARBUS

Portraiture, as can be seen by many of the images in this book, is an intimate business. This is especially so if you work repeatedly with the same person, as I did over a number of years with Morrissey. I do believe that the key to a powerful portrait is, oddly, the symbolic removal of the camera. The subject has to be comfortable enough for their gaze to cross the space between us, to neutralize the barrier of the lens, and to look directly at me, as though the camera does not exist at all. When their gaze hits me in that way, that's exactly how it will hit the viewer. And when that happens, as a photographer, you experience an emotional response, and consequently that emotional response will affect any other observer of the image, too. Fans have told me that they often feel Morrissey is looking directly at them in the portraits I have taken of him.

All portrait photography is, to a certain extent, about pathos. Portraiture preserves something that is finite. The German photographer August Sander captured this idea perfectly when he claimed that portrait photography is about mortification; a person is mobile, they are then frozen in this movement for "a mere five-hundredth of a second of that person's life-time. That's a very meagre or small extract from a life." Just for a moment you seize them in the present, but of course a photograph can only ever reveal the past. The irony is that often the past can appear to be the present because of

this preservation, and it is this paradox that can give many photographs a touch of yearning, of pathos. Many theories of photography describe portraits as being like an inventory of mortality, showing vulnerable lives heading toward their own destruction.

There are a number of elements that I think make a portrait truly articulate, and I've included all of these in this book. An articulate portrait has to convey something about identity, something about self and something about time. Equally, it has to connect to objectification (taking subjects out of themselves) and, in many cases, offer some kind of unexpected reading of the subject. That unexpected reading can either be from me as a photographer, from the subject who sees themselves in an unexpected way, or from the viewer who perhaps reads an unintentional message in the image. Often because portraiture *is* so intimate, it can be a revealing experience for all involved, not least the person being photographed. In a 1975 interview the American photographer Irving Penn said, "Sensitive people faced with the prospect of a camera portrait put on a face they think is the one they would like to show the world…Very often what lies behind the facade is rare and more wonderful than the subject knows or dares to believe." On a more practical level, an effective portrait will also locate itself in time and place, and include effective signs and symbols by which you can read or understand the subject.

These things are sometimes called "props". If you photograph someone in front of a bookshelf, you are making a statement about them, and suggesting they be understood in a certain way. For me as a photographer concerned with building iconography, this use of props is crucial. And once you start using these props, you immediately start making links to issues of identity, self and time.

Morrissey is one of the most collaborative people that I have worked with. He has a strong sense of how he wants to be portrayed, and I do believe he enjoys toying with his own identity and representation. He fully understands how props work and becomes quite playful in how he employs them. When we worked together, he always brought ideas to our shoots. Ultimately the photographer holds the power, and most of my pictures were editorial so my input was quite strong, but that didn't mean collaboration wasn't part of the process. When I photographed Morrissey in his garden, he wanted to include a picture of Terence Stamp behind him in the tree. I was more than happy to do this. The idea was Morrissey's, the execution was mine. The prop was there, and both Morrissey and I played with it.

But with Morrissey, as with anyone else, my main aim is to make the person in my portraits look great. I'm not after a warts-and-all image. I'm willing to work with someone on how a portrait might be constructed but, that said, I don't usually worry if the subject of my photographs likes their

portrait or not. It's more important that I like it, and if I do, I know that fans will, too. A person who has their portrait taken can be the worst judge of what makes the best picture. They are in a position that involves negotiating a number of different, difficult positions. Roland Barthes calls this a "closed field of forces" that intersect and distort one another. When the camera is pointed at them, they are whoever they think they are, the one they want others to think they are, the one the photographer thinks they are, and the one the photographer makes use of to exhibit their art. This is a pretty tricky position to hold, and it is why having some kind of trust between photographer and subject can ease this process considerably.

Morrissey and I shared a similar background, so when it came to representing him and his identity in a particular way, I did at least feel as though I had some insight into him. If I had to state which portrait I felt ultimately did this, it would be one that I deliberately constructed. Curiously, it is a portrait in which you cannot even fully see Morrissey's face – he is in silhouette – and it featured on the cover of my book *Manchester: Looking for the Light through the Pouring Rain*. Morrissey is standing by the edge of the Rochdale Canal on the hump of a cobbled towpath. An iron bridge intersects and frames the top half of the image. It is shot in black and white. Some of the fretwork on the bridge is just visible in the image to the right and left of the frame. Morrissey is standing looking down to the water with his hands in his pockets. I used the light to construct tonal differences, but there is a simplicity to this composition. Morrissey may not have thought that was how it would be shot, but I wanted this image to be emblematic of both Morrissey and the North. I believe there is a timelessness about it in many ways – the iron bridge, the cobbles and Morrissey's noticeable quiff. It could be a still from *A Taste of Honey* or a Billy Fury album cover. But it is undoubtedly Morrissey, and therefore is simultaneously timeless and yet oddly specific. This could not be anyone other than Morrissey. Nothing in a portrait is a matter of irrelevance, whether that's a facial expression, clothing or the surroundings. Portraits are about constructing an identity. I have a strong sense of Morrissey's identity and he has a deep understanding of how visual imagery works. So much so that often with Morrissey, as with this portrait, you don't even need to see his face to know that it is him. A silhouette makes him recognizable enough. You could see a picture of his quiff and know that it is him.

At the same time, I do love the slipperiness of portraiture. In so much as it is possible to capture the essence of someone so that they are recognizable by a silhouette alone, there remains something elusive about it at the same time. Portraits are not really about facts as such but rather constructions. And Barthes remained convinced that it was impossible to capture the essence of a person, the *animula* (the little individual soul). I agree with this to a certain extent, but if you view portraiture as a part of iconography then the "truth" of it becomes less important and the purpose of it more evident. It is an art like anything else, and it requires work.

What I found exciting about working with Morrissey was that he understood and took an active part in where he placed himself in visual culture. In many ways he used images that captured his sound, and this was often my aim when photographing musicians. I wanted to take photographs that would somehow inform a viewer how the band would sound. Morrissey's visual influences take you on an interesting journey – Pat Phoenix, Viv Nicholson, Jean Marais, Yootha Joyce, Shelagh Delaney, Elvis. Then there are the backdrops he uses at his concerts, featuring variously James Dean, Oscar Wilde, Edith Sitwell. What Morrissey does so well is to place himself right in the centre of these influences, so he becomes part of them and they become part of how we think of him.

This links to another essential feature that I think is required for an effective portrait, and that is a strong sense of self. Morrissey plays with his own image in the context of other images, so sometimes we get a picture within a picture, and so on. But to present a sense of self, the portrait needs to have narrative; it needs to tell you something about the subject or give you enough to be able to construct your own narrative. Because Morrissey has an interest in how he presents himself, he was enjoyable to work with. One picture in particular that I think really captures this aspect of him is the one in which he is lying on the floor doing a jigsaw of his own image. I can't remember now whose idea it was to take this photograph, but the jigsaws were a promotional item from the record company for his single "Pregnant for the Last Time". I had one in my bag and I took it out. Morrissey lay on the floor on his left-hand side, looking up into the camera holding a piece of the jigsaw in his right hand. His gaze is direct and bold, and the pieces of the incomplete jigsaw are spread out on the floor beneath him. I think what is happening here is that Morrissey is playing with his own image – both literally and metaphorically. He appears to be toying with people's perception of him and performing some version of himself. It is an almost ludicrous form of narcissism. I love the preposterous idea of him doing a jigsaw puzzle of his own face, creating this multi-mirror-image idea. It offers the viewer a number of readings, and therefore, as an instance of iconography, it is strong. Is Morrissey being tongue in cheek? Is he piecing himself together? What is he up to with that slightly enigmatic side-eye to the viewer? This is more than just capturing a straightforward likeness; the image is making a statement about identity and self.

What then becomes really interesting is that as a piece of iconography an image like this takes on its own life. I want my pictures to be in people's homes, on their walls, on their desks, and often they send photographs to me of my photographs in situ. A common location for my images seems to be in homemade shrines surrounded by Morrissey candles and vases of flowers. My desire to create iconography means that my photographs themselves sometimes literally become a type of secular icon. And I do believe that this elevates the status of the portrait. As with any icon (religious or secular), the purpose is to replace the actual subject, so in people's homes these images become some sort of visual surrogate for Morrissey himself. They seem to be both devotional and celebratory and, perhaps more importantly, they bring pleasure.

Presumably for the viewer there is a sense of intimacy, too, which can really only be achieved if that intimacy is there between the photographer and the subject. Morrissey is very good at breaking down the barrier of the camera and we always felt at ease with each other. This is so crucial for portraits. The French photographer Henri Cartier-Bresson felt that portraits were the most difficult photographs he took: "You have to try and put your camera between the skin of a person and his shirt." For this reason alone, the more you work with the same person, the better portraits you can take.

It also becomes easier to take other risks if there is a trusting relationship between photographer and subject. Objectification plays a large part in portraiture. I don't necessarily mean this in a negative way, though of course lots of portraits do objectify people rather unpleasantly, and this is usually fairly gendered. But what I'm referring to here is the interplay between subject and object, because in portraiture the person in the photograph becomes both: the subject *in* the picture and the object *of* the picture. So sometimes playing around with this can be quite good fun. This is especially so with someone like Morrissey, who inserts himself strongly within his own visual culture and influences.

One portrait that played up to this is the one taken in his garden, featured on the cover of this book. Morrissey is standing in the centre of the frame looking directly at the camera with his head just slightly tilted up and to the left. He is wearing a loose white shirt, uncuffed and open at the neck. Behind him are trees and bushes, and to the left of the frame is a cloud of white smoke. This is what I would call a pure portrait, a classic head-to-waist shot in which Morrissey plays up to the camera. It was a deliberate attempt by me to do a pin-up shot presenting Morrissey in a Hollywood-style portrait. The light is in just the right position, which sculpts his face. You can see this especially around the jawline. Tonally it is lighter around his left ear, falling darker as you cross his face to the

right-hand side. His quiff is quite magnificent. The smoke gives the image depth and the photograph has a Romantic poet, dreamlike quality about it – Rupert Brooke, Keats. The contact sheets for this shoot tell a slightly different story, however. Morrissey thought setting fire to some garden waste would provide some atmospheric smoke, like a dry-ice effect, but it all got out of hand. Some images on the contact sheet show Morrissey completely engulfed by smoke, but luckily it cleared enough to get some really striking shots of him looking great.

That shoot was a good example of things that can go wrong when you're taking portraits. As I've said, Morrissey is full of ideas on shoots, but some of them just won't translate into a picture. Despite this, I was always happy to work around them and give them a go. Getting a great picture can sometimes be about taking those ideas and then suggesting other things, or just slightly modifying them in some way. Other issues lie outside of your control, which can be more difficult to deal with, such as the weather if it's an outside shoot, or the mood of the subject. Sometimes you just have to learn how to make it work despite all of these things, and not let it take up too much time. I have always shot in a sparse and sparing way. Initially, when I first started, this was because I couldn't afford to waste film, but later, even when I was commissioned to do jobs, I was still parsimonious with film, and I remain so with digital images.

Part of this is because I understand the time pressure that well-known people can be under. Their time is important and they often don't have all day to spare waiting for me to get the right shot. I learned quite early on from studying the work of Lord Snowdon that it is a good idea to set up more complicated shots in advance, so that when the subject of the picture turns up you are all ready to go. When Snowdon was shooting the Royal Family, for instance, he'd use stand-ins such as his assistants or editors to pose in the shot the day before so he could work out the composition, the lights and the depth of field. Then when the photographic subject turned up he could simply place them in the shot and take it really quickly. I copied this technique, especially for studio shots, so that sometimes the preparation would take twelve hours but the actual shoot would take ten minutes.

I think that Morrissey understands the power of the image and the fact that it plays a vital cultural role, both in terms of creating his own mythology and cementing a place for him in cultural memory. Most people take photographs to capture a moment and remember it; to preserve it and have it to look back on. Oddly, sometimes what can happen is that people then remember the photograph, not the key moment, so again we see how pictures can be a form of surrogacy. I'd like to think that in our future cultural memory there will be traces of Morrissey informed by my pictures. The art critic John Berger believed that the photograph was unique in this role: "Unlike any other visual image, a photograph is not a rendering, an imitation or an interpretation of its subject, but actually a trace of it. No painting or drawing, however naturalist, belongs to its subject in the way that a photograph does." So in this sense, if we are talking about leaving traces, then we are really seeing how a photograph can offer a spark of immortality to its subject. There will always be something left behind. My pictures of Morrissey freeze him in time, but also, because he is still alive, offer him a future that we now know about. It's because time rolls on in this way that a good portrait does need to anchor itself in time and place. Again, it's that paradox of keeping something still and fixed while it carries on moving.

There are a couple of pictures of Morrissey in this book that do just that. Two of them were taken in Japan in 1991 on the same tour, and both make strong statements about time and place. The first happened as we were outside the Budokan arena in Tokyo. A fan handed Morrissey a present, which contained a homemade T-shirt with a picture of Oscar Wilde and the words "Smiths Is Dead". I'd recently photographed Johnny Marr with a fake tattoo saying "Ex-Smith '82–'87", and Morrissey appreciated the sentiment of this T-shirt. It was like his riposte. He pulled the T-shirt on and I started to shoot. The contact sheet shows that he began by sticking up two fingers, and then he started dancing. One of the images from this shoot included in this book shows Morrissey leaning against the wall with his arms slightly outstretched and his palms facing the camera. He looks serious and I used the light to create a sort of radiant halo around him, which then fades darker into the four corners of the frame. It has the effect of illuminating the upper part of his body, drawing attention to the T-shirt and his face. This was a clear message to fans – The Smiths is dead, get over it. I feel that this was an important moment in Morrissey's visual legacy, where he clearly drew a line under that part of his past. It was time to move on.

The second picture was taken, somewhat inconveniently, in the middle of the road in Tokyo. Morrissey wanted to sit on the floor amid all of the oncoming traffic, but I just wasn't quite prepared to do that with cars and lorries thundering by. We compromised and he placed himself on a traffic island over a grid, though you can see how close the traffic still was. In this image, Morrissey is looking to the left of the frame, smiling slightly, and he has his jacket on the floor beside him. He's wearing a T-shirt featuring Edith Sitwell, which was used as the backdrop on stage during that tour. This portrait is shot in colour, though it is still quite muted and delicate – pale greys, browns and blues. After shooting it I thought it didn't work at all, but now I think the status of this picture has altered and it is now quite a strong portrait.

Part of this has to do with the passing of time and the way the picture represents and captures something that has been and gone. Because it is no longer contemporary, it strongly locates itself in a particular moment, revealing the 1990s truck and cars. It's like a historical document, and again it forms part of a cultural memory. A memorial even, if you will.

The final feature that I think a really articulate portrait needs is some sort of unexpected reading, whether that's by the photographer, the subject or the viewer. One picture of Morrissey in this book that did that for me was taken in Cologne, Germany in May 1991. I'd been photographing the band beneath the Hohenzollern Bridge – one shot of them all together, and then individual shots of each band member. I wanted to take a picture of Morrissey in the same place but he decided to do something different from the rest of the band. We moved to the steps of a footbridge, which were concreted and edged with metal – very urban and sparse. When I photograph Morrissey (or anyone else) I don't really direct my subjects; I'm happy for them to do what makes them comfortable. I expected Morrissey to lean against the railings or something, but what I didn't anticipate as I set up my camera was that he would lie on the floor and pretend to be falling down the steps. If this wasn't surprising enough, what I didn't see was an approaching child walking down the steps toward us, and I actually didn't see him until he came into the frame. I realized I had a split second to capture this, and just as I was pressing the shutter, the kid turned and looked at Morrissey. I really like this picture. Morrissey is in the bottom half of the photograph lying head-first down the steps. He's looking out to the right of the frame, and tonally his quiff looks painterly-black against the grain of the concrete steps. His jacket is falling open and he has a smile on his face. Behind him, the child is looking down at Morrissey with his hand held up to his mouth. You can almost see him wondering what's going on. His right foot is turned toward, and lined up with, Morrissey's ear. For this split second they are sharing the same step, the same space. Morrissey appears oblivious to the child's presence. For me as a photographer this is one of those unexpected, fortuitous occasions. You realize you have just a fleeting moment to capture something that you could never have planned and, if you miss it, you will never be able to capture it again. Even today I have no idea why Morrissey decided to adopt the tumbling-down-the-steps pose, but I'm glad he did as I think this portrait works really well.

There can be other unexpected coincidences with portraits, too, which I think can show how in tune you can be with someone if you share a love of visual culture. Building iconography around musicians means also having an understanding of sound and the ways in which this might be represented visually. I have always wanted people to look at my pictures and have an idea of what a band will sound like based on the way I present them, whether this is Joy Division on a bleak, snowy bridge or Richey Edwards clutching a crucifix, his torso ink-stamped with images of Marilyn Monroe. When I photographed The Smiths in September 1983, I decided that I wanted a rural, arty, Jean Cocteau feel, something that would single them out as sounding different and would reflect the intelligence of those early Smiths songs. In particular, I had in mind Cocteau's Orphic trilogy of films *Orpheus*, *The Blood of a Poet* and *Testament of Orpheus*. I thought the way in which Cocteau used themes of the immortal poet and the power of the mirror reflection would work well with The Smiths, which was emerging as this poetic Northern band creating its own unique sound. I took the band out to Dunham Massey, a large park south-west of Manchester, and found a fountain with a stone-edged pond. You can see from the pictures in this book that I took some shots of the band sitting around the water. From the contact sheet you can also see that I took individual shots of each band member lying reflectively by the pond. Johnny Marr got the idea straight away and lay down while I photographed him, then, after a bit of gentle direction, Mike Joyce and Andy Rourke did the same. Morrissey wanted a different shot from the rest of the band, though, so he crouched down by the water with his arms outstretched. You can see his mirror reflection perfectly in the pool at his feet. In another shot he is lying on his back, holding his hands palms-up to the camera with the round pool behind him thrown into shade. I'm certain that I didn't tell the band I had this Cocteau theme in mind, and they didn't tell me about the forthcoming cover of their single "This Charming Man", which was released the following month. It featured an image chosen by Morrissey of the actor Jean Marais leaning over a pool of water in a still from Cocteau's film *Orpheus*.

Many of my portraits of Morrissey are shot in black and white. This is partly because I have always preferred shooting in black and white, and partly because the final images were mostly published in black and white. The Swiss–American photographer Robert Frank said that "black and white are the colors of photography – to me they symbolize the alternatives of hope and despair…" I like this idea and feel it perfectly sums up the idea that portraits are both about the pathos of mortality and the capturing of immortality, of preserving and celebrating. These two strands run through all of my pictures and are inevitably connected to the notion of time and its passing. I suppose time is not just frozen in the photograph itself but impacts in a practical way on how the portrait is taken.

The techniques, the experience of being photographed, have changed fairly drastically over the last hundred years and continue to change and shift with the advent of digital. Early portraiture was sometimes described as "a mirror with a memory", and this was both metaphorically and literally true. Early portraits were taken as reverse images so that people would see themselves as they did in the mirror. This was how people were used to seeing themselves. Then, when the picture was being taken, you were not able to move for a considerable period of time, so whatever pose and facial expression you adopted would need to be held sometimes for up to 30 seconds. This means that years ago the off-the-cuff shot of Morrissey falling down the steps of the bridge could not have happened. The child would not have been captured – he would have walked through the frame and have been long gone before the picture was taken.

So the developments in photography have changed the nature of portraiture quite significantly, both in scope and execution but, that said, some of the newer techniques are just a different way of doing the same thing. I'm often asked after taking a portrait of someone like Morrissey whether software such as Photoshop has made a difference. Have I become a weird hybrid between a photographer and a painter? My answer is no. Using Photoshop is just like working in a darkroom except you don't get your hands wet. It's also much quicker. And while portraiture is an art, it's not painterly. Unless you want to say portraiture is like painting with light, which sounds a bit pretentious but is actually true. You paint with light to create tone. This is why even portraits that are in silhouette work, and why if you compose your frame well enough people will know who is in the portrait even if the face is not visible. While this may not sound like traditional portraiture, it's one of the ways in which not sticking to the rules can work out quite well. André Kertész, a Hungarian photojournalist, broke every rule – he used unorthodox camera angles and compositions and believed that "a photograph draws its beauty from the truth with which it is marked". He continued: "For this very reason I refuse all the tricks of the trade and professional virtuosity which could make me betray my canon. As soon as I find a subject which interests me, I leave it to the lens to record truthfully." The harsh truth of the camera eye, perhaps?

But there are not just studio portraits. Taking portraits of Morrissey in concert requires a whole different set of skills. It's much quicker, more spontaneous. But even on stage Morrissey uses visual culture in an instantly recognizable way. His tours can be dated by the stage backdrops. And these backdrops are almost always portraits: Harvey Keitel, Edith Sitwell, James Dean. I was able to use these portraits as part of my composition, to pick up everything around Morrissey and then to locate him in space and time. I like the idea of using portraits in this multi-layered way and I think Morrissey understood the power of this type of image, too.

So portraiture really ends up being about so much more than capturing the likeness of somebody's face. It is about playing with time and identity, and ideas of self. It is also about telling a story, sometimes with unexpected outcomes, but never without thought. It is about freezing a person for a moment in history and then celebrating them as they move on into their own future. It has changed and developed over time as techniques move on and rules get broken. Or, in other words, as William Blake said, "What is now proved was once only imagined."

COLOGNE
MAY 1991

ON STAGE

"In musical performances one can sense that the person on stage is having a good time even if they're singing a song about breaking up or being in a bad way. For an actor this would be anathema, it would destroy the illusion, but with singing one can have it both ways. As a singer, you can be transparent and reveal yourself on stage, in that moment, and at the same time be the person whose story is being told in the song. Not too many kinds of performance allow that."

—DAVID BYRNE

There are some major differences between shooting studio portraits and capturing somebody performing live. The main distinction is time. In a studio, you have much more control over both time and subject. You can set up a shot in advance, take as long as you need to get the lights and depth of field just right, and you can try a variety of approaches until you get one that works. On stage, it is completely different. My job is to try to be invisible around the band. You cannot control what is happening and you simply have to shoot what unfolds in front of you, which can often be entirely unpredictable and unexpected.

Sometimes you are restricted as to where you can stand; sometimes you are allowed to shoot only the first two to three songs. I realized early on in my career that there was no point in being subject to such restrictions; you rarely get the shot that you want, and certainly such limitations make it very difficult to capture the spontaneous excitement of live music and the interaction between musicians and fans. The three-song rule shows a complete lack of respect for the photographer. The concert photographer wants to shoot the pinnacle of a gig; to capture the excitement of rock and roll. How are you supposed to do that when the artiste is just warming up? Having a triple-A pass (Access All Areas) doesn't mean you have to shoot everything in sight; it allows you to work unhindered. I'd never have got any of these photos if the three-song rule had been

imposed on me. You can capture the excitement of the live concert only by being able to shoot whenever something happens. On the whole, it simply can't be orchestrated and forced into a particular time slot. There are other changes, too, that have impacted on live photography, not least the use of camera phones in gigs. Whereas professionals might be able to shoot only the first two or three songs, the audience can shoot the entire show, and this is another reason why live photography suffers today.

I also feel that live concert photography is completely undervalued these days. It's seen as juvenilia; as a way of working up to "more serious" areas of photography. Yet in the days before the three-song rule the excitement of the live concert shot was a way of helping to sell an artiste to the public and a way of confirming what their fans knew – that they were hugely exciting (and popular), filling theatres and halls around the world. Great life shots are the lifeblood of rock and roll, and in 2009 the art world welcomed a series of live photographs as part of an exhibition at the Brooklyn Museum, New York, called *Who Shot Rock 'n' Roll*. My picture of Morrissey lying over a monitor taken in the United States in July 1991 was included in this show. This really was recognition from a major gallery that live concert photography is an art form. But it would be difficult for this to happen today, given the restrictions placed on professional photographers.

I never had any restrictions photographing Morrissey on stage, which is why I think my live shots of him are so exciting. Working with someone regularly means that you learn certain ways of photographing the chaos that is taking place on stage. I have never witnessed any other musician who has the sort of onstage relationship that Morrissey does with his fans – from the chanting of his name, to the stage invasions, to the shirt thrown into the crowd at the end of the night. There is something ritualistic and unique about his concerts.

Touring with the same person, as I did with Morrissey on a number of occasions, means that some of the challenges of photographing live concerts can be alleviated. For example, watching somebody night after night, you observe details such as which hand they hold the mic in, whether they mostly look stage left or right, whether they act in a certain way during a certain song, what light is available and when. Once you have this information, it can help you to decide where best to shoot from and anticipate at least certain details in an otherwise unpredictable environment.

And, for me, shooting on stage is about the closest I'll ever get to being in a band. It helps you to appreciate the excitement and the level of adoration, as well as to experience the concert from the band's perspective. Having this privileged viewpoint means that I can then share it with fans. Often when I am on stage with Morrissey, I am looking into the audience and capturing a sea of faces, so that ultimately when they look at my pictures they are able to see what Morrissey sees of them. This subverts the gaze in a really interesting, mirror-image way.

And really this is one of the main purposes of live shots – fans like to see pictures of gigs they have been to. The images spark memories, create pleasure and preserve a powerful moment for them. From my point of view, I get to photograph bands doing what they *do* – playing their own music. Most musicians spend quite a bit of time on tour and on stage, and the physicality of this is exciting. It also gives me an opportunity to photograph the band engaging in all other aspects of touring – so not just playing concerts night after night but doing sound checks, giving interviews, preparing themselves backstage, having a drink afterward. This is a totally different, but no less important, sort of access that gives a more holistic feel to what it means to be on tour.

In July 1991 I accompanied Morrissey and his band on a number of concerts he played in the States, and some of my favourite shots from that time, included in this book, are those taken before the concerts even began. During a sound check at Jones Beach, Long Island, I was able to see Morrissey and the rest of the band in a more relaxed mode on stage, and because it was a sound check I didn't need to worry that I was getting in anybody's way while I took the pictures. The band is much more casual in these moments, there is a quiet energy, and sometimes this is when Morrissey would write the set list for that evening. One picture I really like shows Morrissey lounging on the drum riser surrounded by his band. It has an anticipatory quality about it – we know what is about to happen that night. In another accompanying image, Morrissey is, shall we say, reclining somewhat casually in front of the drum kit, well aware that the camera is on him. The light is perfect in this shot, strongly contouring his face and separating it from the tonal range of the background.

Catching Morrissey unawares was really difficult. Even at a sound check he would know exactly where I was with my camera and where it was pointing – and he was always prepared if it was facing his way. In fact, I think I only ever managed to catch him off-guard once – in the dressing room before a concert in Japan. I was pleased about this because we see a different side to him, more relaxed, less studied, and the pictures are more like snapshots than portraits. I achieved this only because I was changing the film in my camera and I took a few shots as I was reloading to get a light reading. As soon as he heard the camera shutter he looked at me with a mock-disapproving stare, as if I shouldn't have been taking photographs without his knowledge.

In addition to the sound checks, Morrissey would also invite me to other events that happened on and around the tour. One day in Cologne he had to do a series of interviews with the music press and he invited me to stay in the room. I declined his offer, but he informed me that sometimes they could be amusing, and encouraged me to stay. I decided to hang around as the light was really good in the room and I thought it likely I'd get some good portraits. The first interviewer (male) came in dressed like a typical German football fan with beer towels sewn into his denim jacket. He sat down and said, "Hello. So, Mr Morrissey, have you never fancied a fuck?" Morrissey slowly raised an eyebrow, turned to look at the camera, and I took a shot. He never answered the question.

Getting access backstage before and after a concert is fascinating. Spending time with musicians in this area is a privilege. It is proof that there's trust between the artiste and the photographer. I've seen musicians smoking heroin backstage. It's not my job to photograph it. I'm not a paparazzo. I see the dressing room as their space, their home, and I've been invited into their home. I'm not going to be invited back if I betray that trust. Most bands I have photographed like to have a bit of private time before going on stage. They put headphones on and listen to music to get themselves in the "zone". They don't want to be hassled and they certainly don't want me taking pictures of them. Not so with Morrissey. He would set up shoots immediately before gigs and sometimes would have so many ideas that I would worry he was going to be late on stage. Many of the portraits in this book were taken just before he went on – the "Penis mightier than the sword" series, the photo of him with his jigsaw, him holding up the skinhead T-shirt. It seemed almost as though he best prepared himself for a concert with a photo shoot, which I find really interesting, as though having his photo taken relaxed him in some way.

But there is an intimacy that develops when you tour with someone, and this will ultimately feed into the type of pictures that you take. It's important to remember that you're both from different worlds. They're on stage and you're not. That's their world and you're there to document what they're doing. You have to keep the balance right. I always keep a professional relationship. I'm not there to be everyone's friend; I'm there to capture something, a moment in time. It doesn't mean you have to be stand-offish. If I was in the back of a cab with Morrissey, we would have a chat about stuff. But if I was on a train with him and the band, I'd leave him to it, unless I was asked to join in the conversation. I don't have a problem with it; I'm not there to impose myself or start working the room and telling jokes and inviting myself round for Sunday dinner. I don't need to do that. I might take a few pictures, or sometimes not. Morrissey and I would sit at the bar in the evening, maybe, after a gig, and have a chat, or he might go to bed. In Tokyo, he bought me a drink and

asked how my daughter was and we had a normal, friendly conversation. He remembers her name and stuff like that, which sounds quite superficial, but there's a level of intimacy because you are all travelling around together and spending quite a lot of time in the same environment.

Being present at sound checks and interviews and backstage is such a privileged position to be in, but ultimately being on stage during a concert is where the real excitement happens. It is a rare moment of meeting between fans and musician, where one or the other can reach out and literally have (physical) contact. With Morrissey in particular, photographing him on stage further helps to build the iconography and mythology around him. Often he can be dramatic – standing on the monitor, or rather Christlike with his arms thrown wide in a crucifixion pose, his devotees at his feet.

The theatricality of this appeals to me because I have worked a lot in theatre. This means that I approach live photography in a slightly different way from other music photographers, and shoot it in a different way, too. I'm able to encapsulate the wider experience by bringing drama into the shot, including the audience, and using techniques such as shooting into the light. This involves locking light into the borders of your framework and using that as the boundary of your composition. You can't wait forever for the perfect shot. In other words, I compose a photograph on stage: I establish my framework and then whatever passes through my viewfinder is captured. Often with Morrissey this composition can include him, or his distinctive backdrops, other band members – even fans. One photograph I took of Morrissey in New Jersey (on the back cover of this book) shows him mid-flight balancing on the monitor. He is framed by his own backdrop of Harvey Keitel and two band members. Clutching his mic in his right hand, his arms are thrown wide (again, echoes of the crucifixion pose), and his flimsy shirt has ripped open and is trailing from his body, exposing his torso. You get a real sense of movement from this image. Everything looks dynamic and in flux. Plus, in a moment of synchronicity, we have the open mouths of Harvey Keitel, Morrissey and Alain Whyte moving in a diagonal line down through the frame from left to right. There's such energy in this photograph. But it doesn't just happen by chance. Once the composition is in place, I am able to capture what moves into my viewfinder, and to me that is what makes a great live shot. Placing Morrissey in a wider context is crucial. If I just did close-ups, it wouldn't mean anything. I could shoot ten different venues and as a viewer of the image it would be impossible to know where or when they were taken. Once you include the theatrical elements, the signs, the signifiers and the context, the picture tells a completely different story.

As you can see from the images in this book, I much prefer to shoot from the stage. Standing looking up at the band from the pit does not produce as immersive a shot, and I don't really like this angle anyway; it is too restrictive and feels a little removed. Equally, I am not able to give the viewer anything that they cannot see themselves. Being right there in the middle of the band enables me to capture not only the excitement but the audience interaction. Standing in the pit at a Morrissey gig can be a bit precarious anyway – fans have a tendency to use you as stepping stone to get onto the stage, and having someone walk across your head isn't that helpful really.

In the same way as with a studio photograph, you know you've taken a great live shot even before you see it. With everything in place, and if you know the script, you can get yourself in the right position to make this happen. From my point of view, it is not about settling for second best but giving yourself time to capture the perfect moment. Obviously, this is easier if you are on tour with a musician. For example, with Morrissey I soon realized that he often draped himself over the monitor at some point during the gig. So one night I could shoot him from side-stage, the next night I could position myself to shoot him from in front, and another night I might just capture his feet sticking up above the monitor. You can see this in pictures that I took in the United States in July 1991. Morrissey used the monitor to stand on while he was singing and to throw himself over on a stage littered with flowers. In one of these images you can see that everything has been captured in a vertical way. Morrissey's face is not even visible, though it is unmistakably him. He is upside down with his legs stretched upward, dividing the frame centrally through the drum kit in the background. His mic, still held in his hand, is also pointing straight upward, following the line of his leg. The composition draws the eye in this direction, travelling from the bottom of the frame to the top. But what I really like about this image is the playful appearance of Morrissey's left hand, just peeking over the top of the monitor, holding him in place.

So to a certain extent it is possible to try to anticipate what might happen on stage, although that said, every night has something different happening and often this can be down to that magical connection between musician and fans. With Morrissey and his fans, anything can happen. An especially chaotic night was the concert Morrissey played after going solo, at Wolverhampton in December 1988. It was the first time he had performed in public for two years so there was real excitement in the audience and I wanted to capture the love for him and the chaos. Throughout the gig there was a "Morr-i-ssey, Morr-i-ssey, Morr-i-ssey" football chant going on and the flow of people coming on stage was unstoppable. It had been brilliantly managed whereby there was free admission for anybody wearing a Smiths or Morrissey T-shirt. The whole audience was wearing one and this helped to make it an event and create a real sense of community. Even the two women who featured in the "Everyday is Like Sunday" video turned up in matching outfits and I captured them sitting next to each other near the sound desk with Morrissey's quiff resplendent across their chests. There's also a great photo of four young men sitting on the floor in matching *The Queen is Dead* T-shirts, with their arms locked around one another and surrounded by empty beer cans and litter. There was such an atmosphere of camaraderie.

I shot all of the pictures of Morrissey at Wolverhampton standing stage right, by the side of Andy Rourke. When it began kicking off I moved slightly onto the stage, trying not to get in anybody's way because there were ten people trying to climb onto the stage from another angle. The gig was so exciting. It was quite a small stage and I was too close to Andy to get him in shot. Craig Gannon is in the background on a couple of shots. It would have been a nice to do a wide shot of the whole band but ultimately it was a Morrissey gig. As a news photograph, I needed a picture of Morrissey with a fan. That was my focus and my job: to get a lead picture of Morrissey being mobbed. The isolated shot I got shows a lovely relationship between Morrissey and a young man. The central point of this image is the embrace between Morrissey and the fan taking place on a stage covered in wires and leads and flowers. The chaos is palpable, but it also shows almost a moment of stillness. The young man has his head resting in the crook of Morrissey's neck, while Morrissey's hands are pulling down the boy's jacket at the back and on the sleeve. The important element that helped to frame the picture was the security guy. It provides the image with a natural arc – his hand is in shot, kind of holding Morrissey's hair, and you can just make out the edge of his face. There's a real tenderness about every element of this picture.

In many respects, Wolverhampton was like a private gig. The fans' response to Morrissey was overwhelming and I think it was massively encouraged by him because it was being filmed for a live video. It was different from a regular gig. Fans were allowed to do what they wanted. When they climbed on stage the bouncers didn't get heavy with them or give them a kicking backstage. Nobody got thrown out. There was no safety barrier, so it was easy for everybody to get on stage – the relationship with the band and the audience was really close. All this helped my pictures enormously. The fans were part of it, and you can clearly see that. When I shot into the crowd there was just a mass of clamouring hands. In fact, if you look at all my live shots from the 1980s and 1990s, everyone in the audience is looking at and reaching out to Morrissey. Their concentration is aimed solely toward him. I would not be able to get a picture like that today – looking out into an audience now you'd see a wall of camera phones, the backlight illuminating the faces of fans who are mediating their experience through the barrier of a screen, while at the same time capturing poor-quality images and sound.

Luckily, it was not like that at Wolverhampton. Everyone was present in the moment and fully focused on what was happening around them. Morrissey is on record as saying in an interview, "You have to at least from a distance look as though you know what you are doing, and I can manage that", though I think we all came as close as you can to not really knowing what was going on that night. The band had played only eight songs but it seemed like a full gig. It was amazing, but I wouldn't have even heard the songs. I was just getting off on the visual content and the absolute chaos that was unfolding before me. I couldn't have told you what songs they played until I watched the gig back on video a few months later. (They started with "Stop Me If You Think You've Heard This One Before".) When The Smiths split up it was massively disappointing – they had so much potential to still fulfil – but Morrissey's solo career has been astonishing. During that gig, I didn't take any notice of the film crew. I think the still images tell a better story than the video, partly because I was in a more advantageous position than the camera crew, as Morrissey tends to look stage right more than stage left.

The final picture that I took perfectly summed up the whole experience. Outside the venue, the metal barriers used to control the queues lay kicked over and dinted, surrounded by discarded beer bottles, grass and items of clothing – the detritus of a night none of us could have really predicted.

From the start of Morrissey's solo career, in the late 1980s onward, all of us at the *NME* became a bit obsessed with him. In 1991 I had already been on tour with him to Dublin, Cologne and the States, but in September of that year he was due to tour in Japan. I suggested to my editor that I could shoot an on-the-road, reportage-style piece with Morrissey handwriting the captions, though really I just wanted to see the tour. He said, "If you can get him to do it, great." Morrissey said yes.

When I arrived in Tokyo on 29 August, I checked into the hotel and waited for someone to contact me with a schedule. Nobody from Morrissey's entourage had appeared to meet me, and I wasn't quite sure what was going on. I rang reception to ask for various people that I knew were on the tour but was met with a mystified silence from hotel staff. I was told no one with those names had checked in. I finally went down to reception where they gave me a copy of the rooming list. I realized that everyone was listed under the names of various *Coronation Street* and *Carry On* film actors and characters, like Charles Hawtrey, Bernard Bresslaw and Percy Sugden. I later found out that these names had been selected

by Morrissey. I assumed he had taken the name of Eddie Riff because he had a suite and nobody else did. But I never found out who "Jasper C Debussy" was. I went back up to my room and went to bed. The following morning the disquieting silence continued, so I decided I would take some pictures of Tokyo in case we wanted to use any landscapes in the piece. I took the lift down and it stopped two floors below me. Morrissey got in. He said, "Oh, hello Kevin, are we going to do some pictures then?" and off we went. It was as casual and unrestricted as that.

Neither Morrissey nor I spoke Japanese. In Tokyo, it is recommended that you carry a card with the name of your hotel on in English and Japanese so you can give it to a cab driver in case you get lost. But because Morrissey and I just went out, neither of us had our card. Firstly, Morrissey wanted to go to Virgin Records to buy some CDs, despite knowing that people might recognize him in there. And of course as soon as he arrived people were on their phones saying, "Morrissey's in Virgin Records. He's here's now!" Suddenly there was a collective of teenage girls all wanting his autograph. Morrissey managed to buy some T. Rex stuff and then we left, quite rapidly. We got in a cab and, of course, neither of us knew where the hotel was. We both sat in the back just laughing, thinking, "What do we do now?" Then a girl knocked on the window and said, "Do you want to know where you're staying?" I said, "Yeah."

All the fans knew, so she got in the front of the cab and took us back to the hotel. Morrissey just sat there quietly and she didn't say anything.

Morrissey on stage is a very different person from Morrissey off stage. Morrissey on stage will allow people to touch and kiss him. Off stage he's not comfortable with it at all. You can see it with some of the pictures in Tokyo, where he's grimacing or looking embarrassed when somebody has got too close to him. There's a real visceral sense of his discomfort. On stage he's a completely different character, though I remember him saying in a television interview that it's his real self that emerges on stage. He never "performs".

I never witnessed any hostility toward Morrissey from his fans. In fact, in most cases they were completely adoring. As a photographer, this interaction was fascinating. Not only because fans play an integral part (without them there would be no point to the music) but because they offer a level of devotion that visually amounts to some sort of religious gathering. They would bring him flowers as offerings, be desperate to touch the hem of his garment or get on stage with him. His shirt thrown into the crowd at the end of the night took on relic-like status. In Barcelona just a few years ago, fans brought scissors so they could cut the shirt into one-inch squares to share out, almost as if they were getting a piece of him. I know people who have fragments of his shirt framed. For me

with my interest in iconography, this is perfect territory for building a series of images to capture this weird hybrid of secular–religious adoration. A Morrissey concert is about an evening of devotion. And this excitement and love becomes part of the show, like one entity feeding off another. Fans dress like Morrissey, have tattoos etched on their skin, have their hair like his, and stand in line to touch him. Outside the venue I would photograph people who I thought looked interesting, perhaps because of what they were wearing or what they were carrying. Sometimes they would have messages or lyrics written on their skin, so I'd want to photograph the ones who fitted into the visual experience of what I was trying to show, the narrative I was building. And over the years I got to know Morrissey fans; the same people went to see him and they were pleased and happy to be photographed by the person who was photographing Morrissey.

Inside the venue, the singalong that goes on during the gigs captures this devotion and shows fans both in and out of control, fully themselves but allowing themselves to be absorbed into an exterior phenomenon. If you look at any photograph I have taken of the crowds, there are fans reaching out, visibly yearning, utterly immersed in what they are seeing and who they are with. Some faces are agonized with unfulfilled longing; others you can see are deciding whether to risk jumping on stage. There were really poignant moments, too; for example, when Morrissey reached out and a fan managed to just touch the end of his fingers. It must have been quite difficult for Morrissey who sometimes had to carry on singing with a fan clinging onto his leg or draped around his neck. Because I had a wider viewing frame, I could see when something like this was about to happen, but it never seemed to faze Morrissey. He would just carry on singing as if it was the most normal thing in the world to have a fan attached to you. Perhaps it is. Anyway, he didn't seem to mind and on the whole he had very sympathetic security! A picture I took in Japan shows a young woman who managed to get on stage but then was clearly overcome by the experience and was being gently carried off by a bemused-looking security guard.

Capturing this sort of communication is essential and can really only be done by being among the band. Sometimes I'd be able to walk around, which was not difficult as people were always throwing themselves on stage. This for a photographer is an absolute gift. You can watch it unfold and record it. And Morrissey knew how to play his crowd. He wore shirts that easily ripped and had pre-signed tambourines to throw into the audience. And there is real historical importance to these pictures. After 30, 40 or 50 years, I want people to look at my photographs and appreciate how exciting it was to see Morrissey back then. There is continuity – fans have stayed with him

and aged with him. I see fans today at gigs who used to go and see him in The Smiths at the Hacienda back in 1983. And fans are loyal to one another, too. I have a photograph of two 16-year-olds taken at the G-Mex, Manchester, in 1986 who still go to see Morrissey together today. That is loyalty and devotion operating on a number of levels – directed to, between and among Morrissey and his fans.

But everyone was bringing their own stories to the gig. I've only got my stories and they've got theirs. The adoration appeared to come from fans feeling as though Morrissey was singing directly to them, and they identified with this on some deep level. His experiences were their experiences, and this created a powerful bond. There was gratitude and relief that he was saying the words and feeling the things that they had always felt but perhaps had never been able to articulate. The music was everything. This bond was not entirely one-way either. As Morrissey said once in an interview, "The paradox is that I have no love for myself as a human being but have immense pride in the music I make, and believe it has an important place. Others do, too, and the thousands of people with Morrissey tattoos certainly proves something."

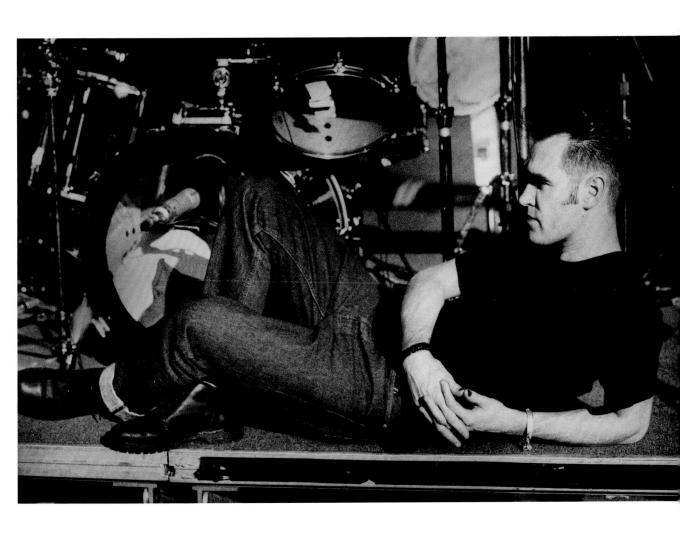

JAPAN
SEPTEMBER 1991

は奉幣の上、新嘗祭に……

四年官幣大社に列せられた。

の御復興のあらまし

造営の社殿は、江戸初期の権現造りの代表的建物として

足されていたが、昭和二十年五月に戦禍に遭い焼失した。

社神道は、大変革を余儀なくされ、混沌たる社会情勢の

興事業は困難を極めたが、氏子崇敬者の赤誠奉仕により

造営」の画期的な大業が企画された。昭和三十三年六月

宗斎行、引続き神門、廻廊、参集殿等が逐次完成、更に

摂社の大修築、神庫校倉の改造等を相次いで竣工し、

昭和四十二年六月奉祝祭が先づ斎行され

けて之を慶賀し、

昭和三十三年六月現社地御鎮座三百年祭が執行された。

一年七月江戸城内御鎮座五百年奉賛会が結成され、五百年

八年大祭を厳修し、昔をしのぶ天下祭にふさわしい山王

『亦の名は山末之大主神　此神は近淡海国の日枝山に野の松尾に坐し鳴鏑を用うる神也』とある。大山咋神は司り、大地を支配し万物の成長発展・産業万うう広大な御神徳は、…王の尊称…を司り給うこと如実である。始元は遙に鎌倉中期に遡る四七八年）太田道灌公が江護神として川越の山王社…

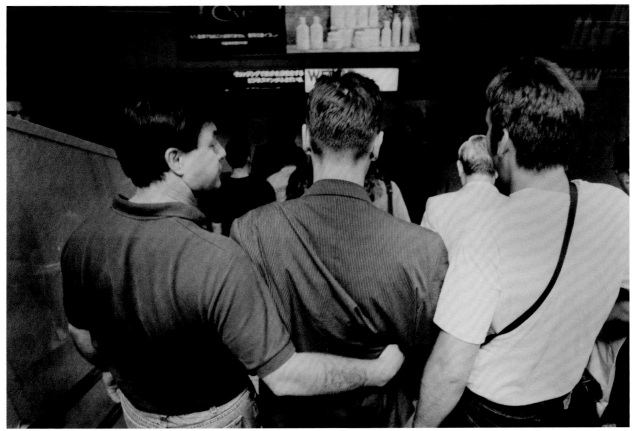

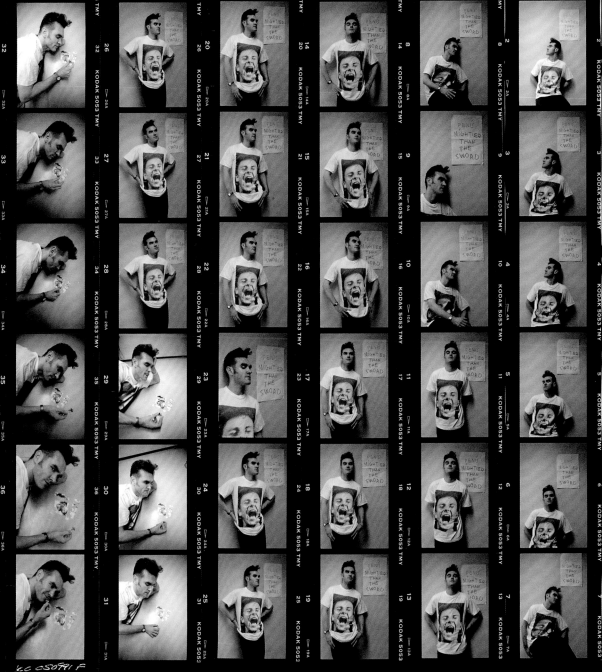

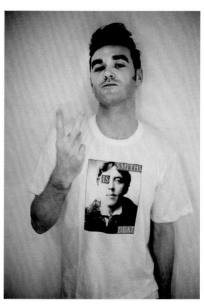

MORRISSEY "KILL

主催　H.I.P　協力　東芝ＥＭＩ株式会社、ロッキング・オン　後援　Jwave

197

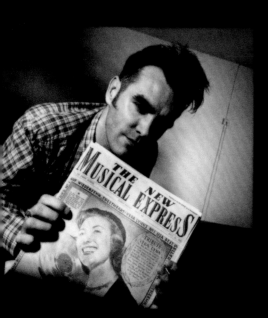

DEVOTIONAL BODIES
BY GAIL CROWTHER

"Wear your heart on your skin in this life ..."

—SYLVIA PLATH

There are very few constants in life. People, objects, places, come and go. But our bodies, symbolically at least, and if we are lucky, remain a constant. And our bodies are encased in skin; a thin, translucent covering, so delicate and fragile and yet more constant than just about anything else. The one thing we cannot escape from is our skin. It stays with us until death and it carries a number of social and cultural meanings. The colour, the texture, the gender, any markings, any limbs missing, hair, no hair, young, old. The body seethes with meaning. We wash it, dress it, decorate it. It is our visual representation of who we are. The body is a site of communication, of expression, and an arena in which we can perceive and be perceived. Our skin entraps us and becomes the spectacle for self-expression. Often we cannot control how our skin is read, but sometimes we can, and in those moments our body becomes a canvas for our identity, both on a personal and a social level. How do we want to read our own bodies and how do we want others to read them? What we put on our skin – branded, carved, inked – carries such significance. "Wear your heart on your skin in this life", says the tattooist in Sylvia Plath's story "The Fifteen-Dollar Eagle". In other words, let the skin that you're in say who you are and what you love.

Tattoos and skin have a long-established relationship. Moving through historical and cultural moments, tattoos have at any one time carried a number of messages: tribalism, clan meaning, belonging, resistance, punishment, love, friendship, devotion. Consequentially, people with tattoos have experienced pride, integration, anger, shame, delight, regret and loyalty. These meanings or emotions are not exclusive; sometimes the boundaries can bleed into each other. The word "tattoo" comes from the Polynesian *tatua*, meaning "to write", and certainly tattoos involve writing on the skin. Yet in the same way that in recent years the word "text" has come to mean more than the written word, we could argue that writing on the skin can involve not just words, but pictures, symbols, numbers, tracings. However, writing on the skin also involves pain, commitment and blood. Every word or picture or symbol is built up by one piercing after another, a needle invading the boundaries of the skin, leaving its mark of permanence. The tattoo is not for the fainthearted, nor for the fleeting emotion. Whether carried out after much research and thought, or whether stamped on the body in a drunken moment, a tattoo is about permanence. You can try to remove it with lasers, but it will always be there, as a faint outline, a trace of what once was, like an imprint on carbon paper, not quite visible, but still very much *there*.

In "Rusholme Ruffians", Morrissey declared that a sign of real, true love is to scratch someone's name on your arm with a fountain pen; the permanence of the ink showing eternal commitment. In a fairly recent phenomenon (roughly over the last

two decades), Morrissey fans have increasingly used their bodies as a site of devotion to the singer. T-shirts, always a visible, outward sign of the type of music you listened to, the type of concerts you went to, became supplemented with a more permanent expression of dedication: the tattoo. And these tattoos differ: song lyrics, portraits of Morrissey's face, etchings over his autograph up an arm, visual representations of a song, embellished patterns. And the placing of the tattoos is also varied: the front of the leg, the back of the neck, across ribs, collarbones, stomachs, wrists, fingers, feet. Fans are offering up their bodies to make a permanent commitment to Morrissey, and the motivations for doing this are unique and personal.

Angie, a 45-year-old fan from Manchester, has "Oh Manchester, so much to answer for" tattooed up the inside of her left arm in black ink. Although she was not born in Manchester, she has lived there for 25 years and she explained how her love of the city and tattoos and Morrissey all converged:

I'd thought about getting a tattoo for a while as I've been a Smiths and Morrissey fan since 1988. I thought long and hard about which one to get, but in the end went with "Oh Manchester, so much to answer for", as I thought it was very fitting due to my love of all things Mancunian, as well as all of the great things that have happened to me since I first stepped foot in Manchester back in 1989. The song that the lyric for my tattoo comes from is obviously based in

great sorrow, but the phrase itself has come to represent Manchester in a very positive light, which is why I wanted to have it on my person.

The body here is used in a celebratory way, combining a love of three things, of which Morrissey is just one part. Interestingly, the lyric Angie chose for her tattoo has been reinterpreted over time, moving from a melancholic lament about the Moors Murders through to representing Manchester in a light of resistance. But Angie has also scripted a personal meaning into this lyric, from a particular moment in her life that she wishes to remember, a time when everything started going right.

Amy, a fan from London, has five Morrissey/Smiths tattoos and plans to have more. Like Angie, she already had a love of tattoos and spent some time thinking about what her first would be. At a particularly striking cultural and historical moment, Amy's decision was made:

The first of the Morrissey tattoos, "There Is A Light That Never Goes Out", I got just after I was 18 and it's on the back of my knee. This was, at the time, my favourite Smiths song. I had always been into tattoos and had been planning it leading up to my 18th birthday. I remember the first time I heard it, I was about 14. I was sitting in a skatepark, up a ramp, in the freezing cold, and someone had The Queen is Dead *and was playing it on an old boombox. The lyrics really spoke to me and I went home and immediately*

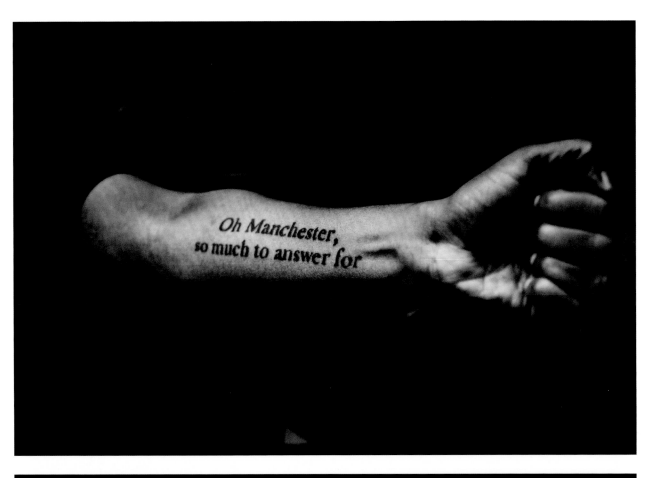

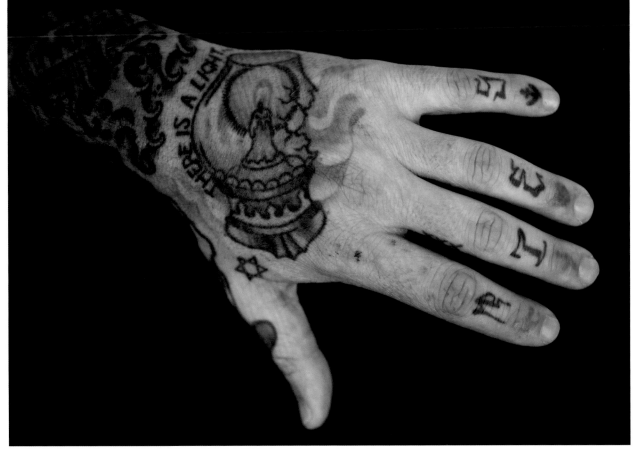

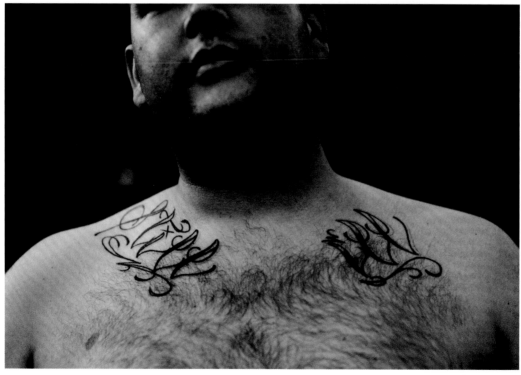

found out everything there was to know about Morrissey. There is something about the way Morrissey writes that, for me, is totally genius, and so heartbreakingly beautiful and honest that from then on, as I got more tattooed, every time a lyric touched me, I added it to the collection.

What appears to be occurring to Amy here is a strong sense of empathy. The honesty that she found in certain lyrics was a source of strength and support and her body is becoming a site of remembrance. She wants to be reminded of the lyrics that touched her, that mean something to her, and she regards these tattoos as a collection of words, highly personal and with meaning.

Joe, an LA-based fan, had a slightly different motivation for his tattoo:

I met Morrissey at LAX Tom Bradley terminal. I got to meet the man himself – it was incredible. It's overwhelming, what do you say to him? I asked for an autograph, which I got on my left arm, then I had it tattooed the next day. I think my tattoo is awesome; the fact that Morrissey himself actually wrote it is awesome.

For Joe, there is a double-layered meaning. Not only does he have a tattoo of Morrissey to express his devotion, but the sketch for the tattoo is drawn personally by the very object of his devotion. This convergence is powerful for Joe because the permanence on his left arm binds him to Morrissey for the rest of his life – or, in Joe's own words, "he will continue to be right here where he always was".

Tattoos can be inextricably linked in a number of ways to notions of personal identity. They say something about who we are, what is important to us and how we want to read our own bodies. Often, they can be an expression of a lived experience or an appreciation of empathy. It could also be said that they are in some way introspection projected outward. The invisible interior of our minds inscribed visibly, outwardly, on the skin. If this is the case, there could be an infinite number of reasons why people choose certain tattoos and the meanings that they ascribe to them.

But what is occurring between Morrissey and a fan that results in such an expression of love and loyalty? A field of literature on fandom studies is increasing all of the time, but given the scale of the phenomenon there is actually relatively little written about it – and even less exploring the nature and variety of affection and attachments that manifest in people's lives. How and why do we invest value and meaning in another person? What is the process by which we choose who this other person will be? Sociological thought suggests there is a direct link between psychological and social conditions. We live in a fragmented, modern society that increasingly isolates people from any real sense of community. The result of this is a fragmented and incomplete modern self. A self that requires some form of comfort and compensation to make up for everything that it lacks in contemporary life. It can be no surprise

that the theme of many Morrissey songs reflects this isolation and sense of loneliness, an inability to fit into the paltry offerings of a world that seems to shame and exclude. So some fans who identify with Morrissey may feel a sense of empathy, but equally they may feel their isolation a little alleviated. They may detect someone who they perceive as being just like them, as though the sentiments of Morrissey's lyrics have sprung straight out of their heads, offering the comfort of familiarity, a sense of recognition.

Yet another key aspect of fandom that should not be overlooked is the amount of pleasure and creativity it can bring. Fans love Morrissey because they love his songs, and his songs form a sonic backdrop to their lives. Most remember where they were the first time they heard him singing. Most have a significant moment when one song had a profound effect. They were indeed the songs that saved their lives in all sorts of ways.

The repetition of certain lines of poetry or songs or prose can have a powerful effect. The first time we read something we can be struck by the truth and perception of it. It can then become like a mantra, an utterance, that we can use either as a reminder, or even for strength. One of the most popular Morrissey tattoos is the song title "There Is a Light That Never Goes Out", a phrase that surely encapsulates the very essence of hope. How meaning is then attached to these words is often highly personal. For fans, the stories behind their decision to get these words tattooed are varied. Sometimes it can be in remembrance of a loved one who has died, or sometimes the end of a relationship, or even managing to escape an abusive situation. The skin then becomes a monument, a memorial, upon which something is etched that can never be taken away. This permanence shows itself in two ways. First, there is the actual physical existence of the tattoo that a person will take to the grave. Second, often the message of the lyrics or song title is about establishing a type of permanence: "There Is a Light That Never Goes Out", "Still Ill", "Don't Lose Faith". What tattoos achieve is the freezing of a cultural moment, which again offers durability and memorialization. Tattoos do not allow us to forget.

As we have seen, often that frozen moment can be about support and pleasure, the remembrance of a happy time but, equally, troubling periods can be captured, too. Amy chose to etch upon her body a disturbing time in her life, as though remembering the bad times is just as important as remembering the happier times:

I have a strange relationship with the album Vauxhall & I *because it reminds me of a bad time in my life and so I tend not to listen to it very much anymore. Nevertheless, "Why Don't You Find Out for Yourself" remains in my top Morrissey songs. I got "Sick Down to My Heart" tattooed across my collarbone in 2010.*

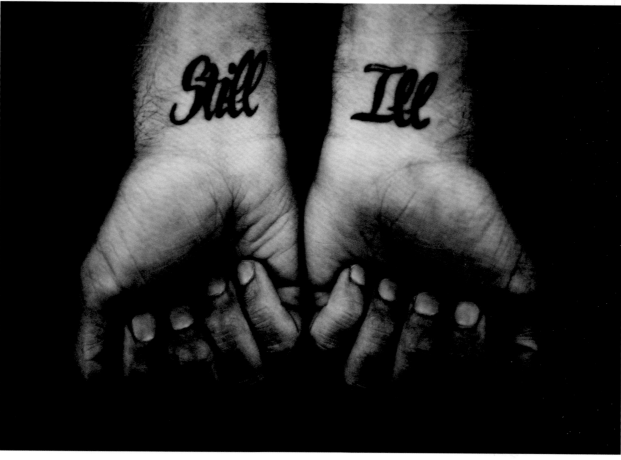

There are other explanations, though. Infinite explanations. Morrissey fans become active producers of a text, creating their own meaning that is tied up with a range of emotions. Some fans associate tattoos with anniversaries, births, deaths, mourning, the end of a relationship, the start of a relationship, or to seal a friendship or say goodbye. Any significant life moment or emotion can be captured and immortalized.

Sometimes this moment can be captured on a number of platforms, like an infinity mirror, reflecting itself repeatedly. Joe, whose tattoo was written on his arm by Morrissey, explains what else happened during this meeting: "I asked for a picture and got one, as well as some video with him." So not only did Joe engrave an autograph permanently into his skin, he also took a photograph of himself with Morrissey, along with video footage. But following this he then had his tattoo photographed while he was holding the picture of himself meeting Morrissey at the point that the arm inscription occurred. This is a fascinating freezing of a moment replicating itself on a series of levels.

The personal nature of an attachment to Morrissey and the decision to etch his words or picture into the skin is undoubtedly speaking to an individual sense of self. But in so much as tattoos are about personal identity, equally we can see they are inevitably about social identity as well. We may read our own bodies, but other people read them, too. Sometimes our social characteristics mean that we cannot control how our bodies are perceived. They inhabit an already existing social structure dictated by features such as gender, ethnicity, age, class, disability. Preconceptions and stereotypes inform how we read bodies, and this is where the history of tattoos becomes interesting, because they have traditionally been used for a number of different purposes over time, and many of those uses are still relevant today, if in a slightly modified form.

One key feature of the *tatua* was to write on the skin in order to denote belonging. Certain markings would indicate a particular kinship and collectivity. Anybody looking at these tattoos would know where a person belonged and who they were. In contemporary culture, although in certain parts of the world this purpose still exists, we could argue that, in the context of Morrissey fans, the desire to express a certain kinship is also present. Certainly, a Morrissey tattoo has deep personal significance, but it also often exists to be read by others, like the wearing of a T-shirt or a badge. If it is on display, it invites a reading and it transmits certain messages about that person with the tattoo – their likes and dislikes, perhaps even their values and ideals. The individual body then forms a social body, a fan collectivity and thus subsequently can create a sense of belonging.

Perhaps this is not so surprising given the commonality of experience voiced by Morrissey

fans who are drawn to his words and songs by a perceived shared sense of isolation, detachment and feeling like an outsider. In a fragmented world filled with a sense of not fitting in, using the body as a platform for self-expression, to be read by similar-minded people, can reduce that sense of exclusion. And the shock of recognition can be a comfort as well – seeing words or a face that you know offers the consolation of familiarity. Although previously Amy spoke about remembering bad times via her tattoos, she equally recognizes the importance of this sense of belonging:

Listening to any album, Smiths or solo, is so familiar and comforting, as though the albums were old friends. Something about the way Morrissey writes just captivated me from the moment I heard it, and I think when it comes to Moz, once you're in, you're in! In my eyes, the man can do no wrong! I also love that at gigs there is an overpoweringly strong sense of mutual love and appreciation for him, which brings everyone together.

This sense of community that is so important to Amy is also expressed via groups such as the Moz Army and Morrissey conventions and tribute evenings, in which people can meet and share their love for all things Morrissey. There is a strong online collective, too – a number of forums where people can come together for discussions, complaints, arguments and appreciation. Images of tattoos can be shared on Twitter, Instagram, Facebook, Pinterest and blogs. Fans can swap stories and offer recommendations. And while these stories and fan motivations are diverse, there is, nevertheless, for some fans, a sense of collective identity even amid this lack of homogeneity.

This collective identity extends from fans to Morrissey, too, who some perceive as sharing their struggles and feelings of displacement. Again, these experiences can be diverse. One example is summed up by Angie, who grew up in the 1970s and 1980s in Huddersfield:

I was, to add to my list of woes, a bit of a loner and a weirdo at school, stayed in and read a lot due to very strict parentage, which meant that books were an essential form of escape for me, didn't have many friends, wore glasses from the age of 12, was bullied mercilessly and wasn't at all popular. I believe Morrissey had a similar experience growing up (apart from his parents providing a lot more freedom), so again I can relate to this totally.

There is a strong sense of identification and shared, lived experience expressed here. Perhaps, given Angie's experiences growing up, it is not so surprising that the first tattoo she had was a place, a city, in which she could belong.

Another traditional use for tattoos was resistance – flouting cultural norms, creating a subculture of decorated bodies to be frowned upon and judged as abject. Today, tattoos are

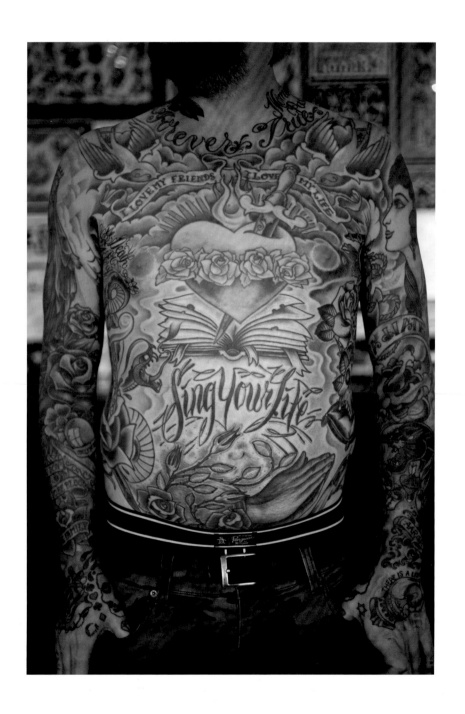

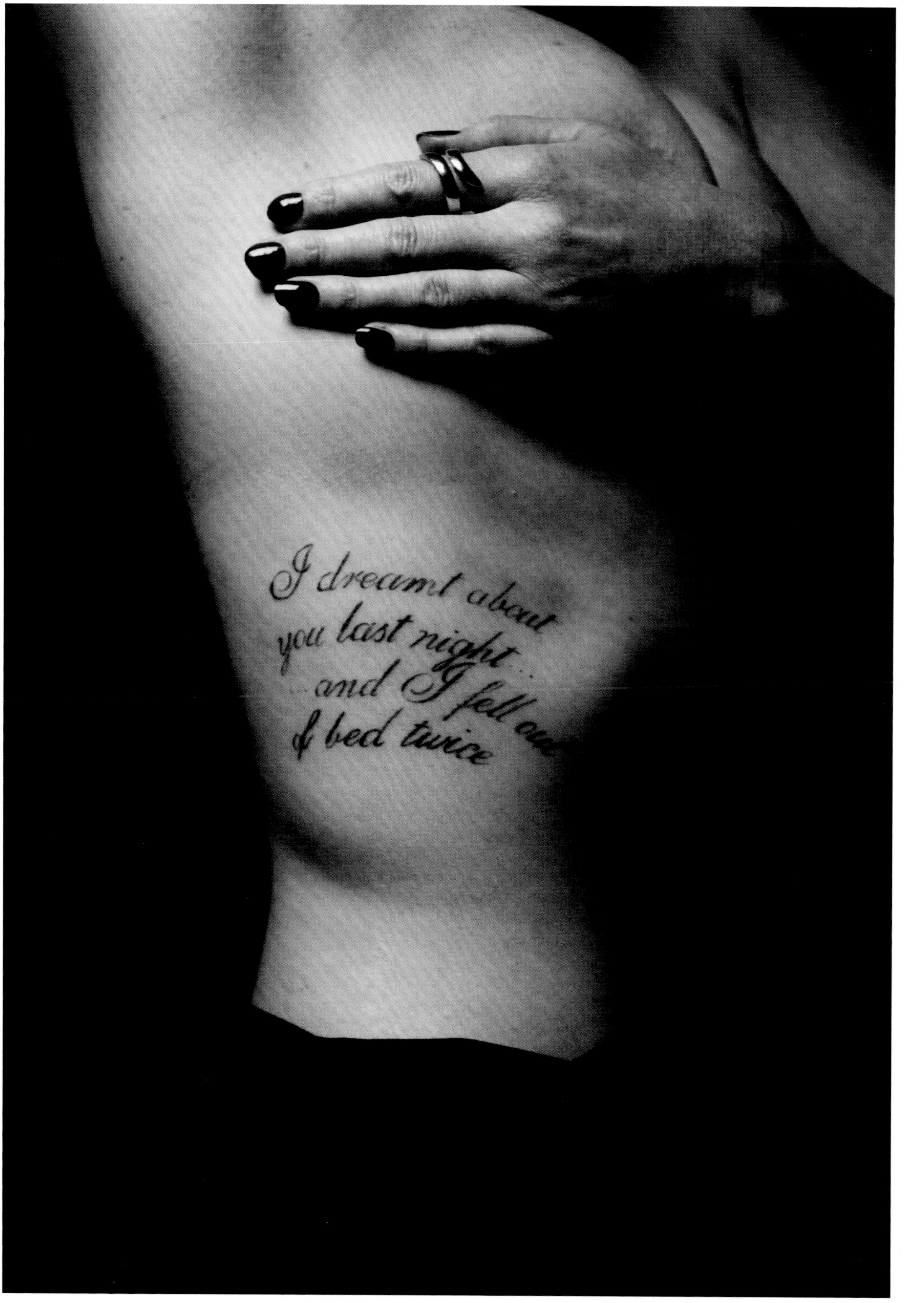
I dreamt about
you last night...
...and I fell ou
f bed twice

arguably much more mainstream, especially since the 1990s onward. Yet they still have the power to shock or to disrupt social expectations. They can also surprise the gaze. *Where* on the body people choose to get tattooed is significant, in particular whether the tattoo can be covered up or hidden or whether it will be permanently on display, for example on the face. Then *what* gets tattooed is important: the defiance of "Life is a Pigsty", "Hated for Loving", "Maladjusted" or "Do You Hate Me?" Confrontational words of resistance celebrating difference and a refusal to conform. It could be argued that fans – any fans – discriminate fiercely by clearly marking the boundaries between themselves and the rest of the world. The obvious barrier between our self and the rest of the world is our body, our skin. Any resistance, any statement we want to make, could understandably be most powerfully made by leaving it permanently on this site. The body becomes a visual canvas heaving with meaning and carving out its place in a cultural environment.

But being a Morrissey fan involves toying with all sorts of boundaries, in the same way that the content of Smiths and Morrissey songs do. Rather than Morrissey's fan base being narrow and of a particular cultural location, it transcends certain confines to include all, regardless of gender, sexuality, ethnicity. In fact, the content of many songs that address being an outsider might especially appeal to those in marginalized groups of society. Do themes of isolation and rejection transcend social characteristics? A Latino Morrissey fan based in Los Angeles combines place/location with the man himself, merging them into a shoulder tattoo that reads "Moz Angeles". And being part of a minority group once again raises issues of belonging or rejection. The sense of community created by Smiths songs and Morrissey's words becomes something that fans protect fiercely. And the policing of who should and shouldn't be able to be a fan was perhaps best evinced when a Conservative ex-Prime Minister of the UK, David Cameron, declared himself a Smiths fan. That such a mismatch could occur was met with universal horror. And not just from fans. Johnny Marr banned David Cameron from liking The Smiths.

So boundaries that are crossed and maintained play an important role in establishing a fan collectivity. Perhaps the example with David Cameron shows not that certain people *can't* be Smiths fans, but rather asks the question, why would they *want* to be? The weird paradox of being a Morrissey fan sometimes comes from an aloneness in a collective – a sense of isolation alongside the relief that you are not the only one who is isolated. Amy recognized this in herself with one choice of tattoo:

I have "How Soon is Now", on my wrist, I cannot begin to count how many times I have listened to that track, "There's a club that you'd like to go

...And you go home and you cry and you want to die." Throughout my youth I experienced this exact experience, as I'm sure many did. I don't claim to be original and when I heard those lyrics for the first time – though it sounds cheesy – I cried, because it was so pertinent.

The strong emotional reaction to this song appears to be both highly personal (it's what Amy lived through) while at the same time acknowledging that she is not alone, that there is nothing original about her response.

Angie had the intersection of a number of issues to deal with while she was growing up:

My parents hail from the West Indies (Aruba and Grenada, to be precise), and the parents of the individual members of The Smiths all originate from the Republic of Ireland (apart from Andy Rourke's mother, who I believe is English), so as the child of fellow émigrés I feel there is a massive connection. It's that sense of displacement also in that I was born and bred in a certain area in a particular country, but was never made to feel like I was actually from that place due to my ethnicity and cultural background, which I know Morrissey also went through.

Amy and Angie's social rejection illustrates how they used Morrissey as a source of support. Other fans speak of, for example, how the gender neutrality of many Morrissey lyrics helps them to make sense of a confused sense of sexuality, the obliqueness

giving them space to consider the role of desire. Fans who are animal rightists identify with the politics of "Meat is Murder", or "The Bullfighter Dies". Men rejecting the dominant discourse of masculinity find comfort in songs such as "I'm Not a Man", and those trapped in the uneventful humdrum towns where the rain always falls embrace the sentiments of "Everyday is Like Sunday".

Yet if, as some fans claim, it feels as though Morrissey is writing their lives, what happens if this goes awry? And what happens if it goes awry and you have a permanent branding of his face or words somewhere on your body? This is surely one of the greatest dangers of an emotional attachment to a living person. At some stage they may end up disappointing you. Morrissey, who on several occasions has indicated "everything" is in the songs, repeatedly sings about how unlovable he is. On the whole fans disagree. But sometimes they do fall out of love with him, and, as ever, boundaries bleed. Love is so close to hate. Strong attachments can be volatile and subject to change, and when you offer up devotion, if something goes wrong, the impact can be devastating. By his own admission, Morrissey regards himself as having something to say, and in an increasingly bland music industry he observes that it is not difficult to be controversial or to sound outspoken. If you happen to agree with what he says, this can be exhilarating. If you happen to be offended by what he says, it can be shattering.

Fans with tattoos who disagree with some of Morrissey's pronouncements appear to have a number of different strategies for dealing with him. One is to have a chronological cut-off point where they will not engage with Morrissey after a specific date. They love him and remain in love with him up to a certain point in time, and then end their association after that point, as if he no longer exists. Their tattoo therefore reflects that particular moment and they remain comfortable inhabiting a past in which Morrissey remains the Morrissey that they loved. Another tactic is to retain their attachment to Morrissey but with an air of disappointment. He remains important in their lives, but with his dazzle a little dimmed. Their tattoos are still an integral part of them and how they feel about him, though often they would not plan any future Morrissey tattoos.

In similar fashion, some fans fall out of love, find some of his behaviour unforgiveable, let time mellow and then gravitate back toward him at a later stage. This is the situation that Angie finds herself in now, having taken a long hiatus from Morrissey due to a distressing incident at a Smiths night in Manchester in 1995. Being of British Afro-Caribbean background, she reluctantly found herself dancing to "The National Front Disco", during which she was subjected to a racist incident that left her profoundly shaken. She explained:

Even though I am fully aware that "The National Front Disco" does NOT glorify that horrific neo-Nazi organization and in fact seeks to do the exact opposite, I still held Morrissey vicariously liable for the sheer torment and upset I was subjected to on that most horrendous of nights, and if I am totally honest I have never really forgiven him for this.

It is hardly surprising that, when an attachment which previously brought so much inclusion and comfort turns into the exact opposite, the impact is severe. Angie did not go to a Morrissey concert for 21 years, but in 2016 she felt enough time had passed for her to return. She did not buy a Morrissey album for 20 years but has just bought *Low in High School*. She feels the passing of time has mellowed her anger and anguish. She has never, however, regretted her tattoo and would never consider removing it:

Although I sometimes despair of Morrissey, the tattoo is something that I knew I would be happy with forever, and this is still the case. Although I am not originally from Manchester, it is in my blood and will always mean such a great deal to me.

One tactic that Angie has recently employed is one that others have long relied on to retain their attachment to Morrissey in the face of disapproval or disappointment – and that is separating the musician from the music. There is a long-standing debate in the arts regarding exactly what sort of connections we should draw between an artist and their work. If a painter transgresses moral

boundaries, should we still appreciate their art? If a writer acts appallingly, can we still like their work? Some Morrissey fans draw this distinction to allow some distance between a man they have usually never met and don't know, and his lyrical and musical output. By forming an attachment to the work, they can sidestep any difficulties should Morrissey himself say anything that offends them. Equally, any misdemeanour on his part does not affect the choice of lyric they may have tattooed upon them.

Amy, and others, draw a different sort of distinction, however. For example, Amy does not feel it is possible for her to separate Morrissey and the music "because Morrissey IS the music". The difference for her comes between Morrissey the person and Morrissey the musician, arguing that an onstage persona is all that she and most other Morrissey fans actually have. Equally, she is clear that musicians are not politicians and neither do the views of any musicians sway her own:

I get asked all the time by friends and colleagues what I think of Morrissey's latest controversial remark, and they joke about me being "Morrissey's biggest defender" but I really try to, even if this is naive of me, stay devoted to Morrissey the artist/musician/ performer and not get caught up in his personal views. I have my political and moral views and they are not influenced by the views of musicians.

The boundaries are clearly drawn and they do not get transgressed. With this in mind, far from regretting her decision to have five Morrissey tattoos, she is planning to add future ones.

A final response to a fractured attachment to Morrissey is to sever all contact with his music, to no longer attend concerts or buy albums, and to remove existing tattoos either by laser treatment or to cover them up with other tattoos. For one fan, his disappointment was so great, he could no longer bear to have the lyrics on his skin.

Bodies, however, remain our main conduit for communicating with the world. We read and are read. Our skin sheds and changes, ages and alters. But it contains us and we cannot escape it. The marks we choose to make upon our skin are powerful statements because they carve us out as individuals. The ink which settles into the very cells of the skin becomes an indelible watermark. And ultimately it is about devotion and devotional bodies. It is a declaration; it is forming a bond, and recognizing the permanence of that bond. Morrissey has provided many people with a textual framework for their life, words that they can live by and imbue with their own meaning. Poetical mantras of remembrance and hope. Wear your heart on your skin in this life, and then take it to the grave.

Dr Gail Crowther is a feminist sociologist specializing in the life and work of Sylvia Plath, archival studies, and fan cultures. She engages with the politics of gender, power, and animal rights.

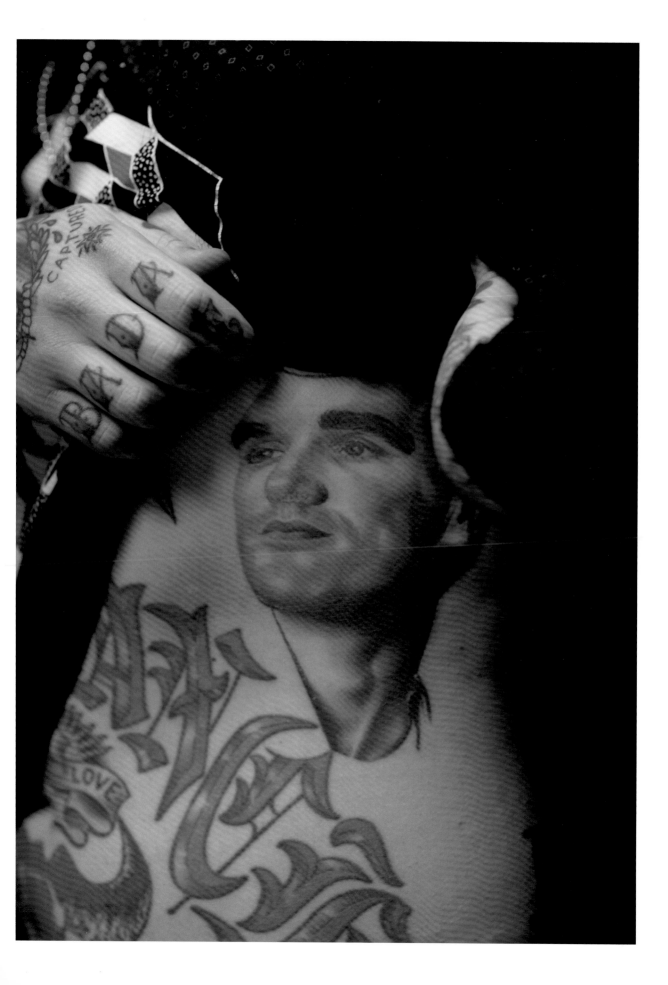

ACKNOWLEDGEMENTS

Thanks to my agent Carrie Kania at C&W for believing in my idea for the book and to Joe Cottington at Octopus for realising it.

Thanks also to Pauline Bache and Jonathan Christie and all the team for turning it into something of which I'm immensely proud.

Also to Gail Crowther for her clarity, vision, intelligence and extreme patience in turning my mumblings about photography into erudite prose.

Thanks also to the ever patient Julian Ridgway and the team at Getty Images for all the excellent scans and for putting up with my eternal requests for "Just one more".

Thanks are also due to Shaun O'Donnell, Julie Hamill, Sally Williams and my daughter Ella.

Finally I've worked on the fan tattoo photographs for the past six years and met lots of lovely people along the way. Sorry I couldn't include everybody and I understand that *Sorry Doesn't Help*, but I hope you all enjoyed being part of the process.

An Hachette UK Company
www.hachette.co.uk

First published in Great Britain in 2018 by Cassell, an imprint of Octopus Publishing Group Ltd
Carmelite House, 50 Victoria Embankment, London EC4Y 0DZ
www.octopusbooks.co.uk

Photographs and text copyright © Kevin Cummins 2018
"Devotional Bodies" text copyright © Gail Crowther 2018
Design and layout copyright © Octopus Publishing Group 2018

Distributed in the US by Hachette Book Group
1290 Avenue of the Americas, 4th and 5th Floors, New York, NY 10104

Distributed in Canada by Canadian Manda Group
664 Annette St., Toronto, Ontario, Canada M6S 2C8

ISBN 978-1-78840-023-7

A CIP catalogue record for this book is available from the British Library.

Printed and bound in China

10 9 8 7 6 5 4 3 2 1

Commissioning Editor: Joe Cottington
Senior Editor: Pauline Bache
Additional text: Gail Crowther
Copyeditor: Helena Caldon
Creative Director: Jonathan Christie
Senior Production Manager: Katherine Hockley